ADVANCE PRAISE

"The Next Normal is a must-read for anyone who wants to create a team and organization that values leadership, empowerment, and accountability. In an approachable and lighthearted manner, Greg combines first principles of leadership and change with a practical and actionable team management system that can scale to renew your organization."

—**MARSHALL GOLDSMITH**, author of the *New York Times* bestseller *Triggers*

"My job as a leader is to make things better for the organization, my team, and each person. Greg's coaching helps me set my teams up for success. His lessons are simple and straightforward. And he's put it all in this book."

—**TODD BURGER**, Chief Experience Officer, AAA Northern California, Nevada, & Utah

"Greg's coaching and work with our leaders and teams helped us design and deliver significant transformation and results again and again. The Next Normal is a must-read for anyone who knows the status quo will not achieve the results they seek. Greg provides an approachable, actionable, and proven system for leaders to challenge the old norms and empower their teams to make positive change."

—**JOHN MCKENNY**, Senior Vice President and General Manager, BMC Intelligent Z Optimization and Transformation

"This should be required reading for first-time leaders, long-time leaders, and everyone in between. It's invaluable advice and terrific coaching in book form."

—**JANET WIDMANN**, President and CEO, Kids Care Dental & Orthodontics

"COVID changed the world! In The Next Normal, Greg Giuliano reminds us that leaders are disruptors who create the future. He provides an approachable, actionable way for leaders to succeed in challenging the status quo and enabling positive transformation."

—**ROBERT RIGBY-HALL**, Chief People Officer, Orveon Global

"When I read The Next Normal, I could hear Greg talking to me. His advice and coaching have never failed me. His book delivers too. In it, he asks leaders to think deeply and differently about the 'next normal' they have the power, agency, and responsibility to create. Greg never lets you forget, you have agency. Everything you do is a choice. Let's make the right next choices."

—**CAROLYN HENRY**, Vice President Field Marketing, Fortune 500 Technology Company

"For leaders looking to drive transformational change for their organizations, The Next Normal is a must-read. Greg draws on his decades of experience as an executive coach to help leaders uncover how macro-level outward change starts with a micro-level inward focus. This is the perfect book for the intentional leader."

—**ARTHUR WOODS**, Co-Founder at Mathison and author of *Hiring for Diversity*

"As a coach, Greg drops truth bombs and asks hard questions. He does this in person. He does it in The Next Normal. Take them both on your leadership journey."

—**BRIDGET BISNETTE**, former SVP Global Channel Sales, Programs, and Operations at Riverbed Technology. Now President at Bisnette GTM Services

"Even the title is a reminder! What's normal is up to me. What's next is up to me. Greg provides a way to make it real."

—JEVON MCCORMICK, President & CEO at Scribe Media, author of *I Got There*

"Greg has an insatiable curiosity to understand how we all can become better leaders in a fast-changing world. In The Next Normal, Greg challenges our preconceptions of leadership and lays out a way to realign our focus for the future. A must-read for established and aspiring leaders alike."

—IAN SYMES, Executive Vice President, Right Management

"Greg gets leaders and teams moving together. In The Next Normal, he describes a systematic approach to leadership that's so clear it sparkles. Every page provokes insights and jump-starts action."

—MICHAEL CROTON, Albion Communication

"In The Next Normal, my brother Greg's two decades of experience making leadership concepts real for leaders moves beyond theory to implementation and action. His insights and approaches to leadership have been helping leaders strengthen their teams and organizational outcomes for years. As a former mayor now leading a CEO business roundtable, I know firsthand The Next Normal will be a trusted guide for the reader's leadership journey."

—NEIL G. GIULIANO, President and CEO, Greater Phoenix Leadership

THE
NEXT
NORMAL

THE
NEXT
NORMAL

TRANSFORM YOUR LEADERSHIP,
YOUR TEAM, AND YOUR ORGANIZATION

GREG GIULIANO

Bestselling Author of *Ultra Leadership*

LIONCREST
PUBLISHING

THE NEXT NORMAL

Transform Your Leadership, Your Team, and Your Organization

ISBN	978-1-5445-3001-7	*Hardcover*
	978-1-5445-3000-0	*Paperback*
	978-1-5445-3002-4	*Ebook*
	978-1-5445-3205-9	*Audiobook*

For those leaders who go to the edge and push farther.

"Let us not return to what was normal,
but reach toward what is next."

—From "A New Day's Lyric" by Amanda Gorman

CONTENTS

FOREWORD

CHRIS KAY, EVP, CONSUMER AND BUSINESS
BANKING, MARKETING, M&T BANK

I MET GREG GIULIANO FOR THE FIRST TIME on a foggy morning at Cavallo Point, perched at the foot of San Francisco's Golden Gate Bridge. We shook hands, exchanged pleasantries, then embarked on a picturesque walk to discuss where I wanted to go—as a leader.

So began a much longer journey of discovery about my leadership impact and the work I needed to do to become a servant leader who helps people and teams achieve bold and purposeful goals.

As our collective customer and employee expectations change at an ever-increasing pace, we as leaders need to help build and sustain more adaptive organizations, as well as keenly understand our role in creating a strategic culture shift—one that transforms ourselves, our teams, and our organizations in the process.

In *The Next Normal*, Greg lays out the change we, as leaders, need to embrace and provides space for our introspection and discovery. He believes that rethinking, resetting, and renewing our leadership can ensure our next normal will be a step forward. It can galvanize our teams so they're aligned on what's most important and able to achieve their best in an environment of empowerment and accountability.

Like many leaders, I often gloss over the action items in books on leadership, favoring the insights and lessons over action. In *The Next Normal*, Greg makes the case that taking a systematic approach to lead change at scale is imperative and achievable. Throughout the following pages, he outlines a team management system that starts with impactful leadership to ensure alignment and empower our teams to maximize their potential and, in turn, achieve big things. That's one element that makes this book a thoughtful roadmap to drive business and cultural transformation. The team I lead has been building our capacity to coalesce around the mantra of "lead change together," using the methodology shared by Greg. In support of clear and refined outcomes, legions of 21st-century leaders are defining Team Roadmaps, devising action plans, and convening coaching conversations on how to unlock speed and impact, all rooted in one foundational belief: with proper preparation and execution, we can better unlock the creative talent of those we lead.

This is the direction Greg's work provides, all while provoking questions about the role of management, leadership, and changes happening every day. For me, it provides a helpful reminder of the continued work I need to do to become the leader I strive to be but also brings me back to that misty morning walk overlooking the San Francisco Bay. That was a core moment in my current leadership journey and reminds me that, for many, their discovery is still evolving—or just beginning.

Wherever you are, use Greg's work as your necessary traveling companion to a more strategic style of leadership—and enjoy the ride.

INTRODUCTION

THE POINT OF NO RETURN

SOMETIMES CHANGE HAPPENS TO US, and sometimes change happens because of us.

The COVID-19 pandemic happened to all of us. The world has changed, and the effects will last a generation. Some long for life as it was in the "before times" and focus all their energy on trying to return to a world that no longer exists. Others resign themselves to this new reality while asking, *Why me?* and *How do I survive this?* when things don't go how they'd like.

These reactions are normal. COVID-19 disrupted the order of things, swept away people's certainty, and provoked a search for the meaning of it all. We felt out of control because, to a large degree, we were. In short, our lives were threatened.

If that sounds hyperbolic, it isn't. We are order-seeking, meaning-seeking beings. When our certainty or control is threatened, the oldest, most primitive part of our brains is activated. Our visceral, instinctive reaction is to fight, take flight, or freeze. Layered on top of this instinctual reaction are the emotions that attach themselves to our experience of being and feeling threatened. Fright can trigger anger or sadness, which can drive our decisions if we allow it.

Organizational change professionals like to say people don't fear change; people fear loss. There's a degree of truth in that: when faced with change, we fear losing our sense of control. We know where everything is. We know how everything works. We know what's expected of us. We know how to survive in our status quo, our comfort zone. When that all gets disrupted, what do we do?

Some people expend enormous amounts of energy and time trying to change the past—for part of my life, I was one of them. I still have to remind myself how that is a colossal waste of time. There's no going back. There's no stopping now. As a leader, you have to constantly ask yourself, *Am I going to lead today or not?* This book is for those who choose to lead.

The point of no return is the moment in your journey when the option of turning back is no longer available to you. Effective leaders know we are always at the point of no return. You're continually faced with increasing demands for your time and attention, and the pace isn't going to let up. If you stay in the game, you've got to keep playing.

While the COVID-19 pandemic caused major disruption across the globe, it also provided a point-of-no-return opportunity for leadership. Some long-overdue decisions about how to go to market or how to run a business were no longer avoidable. Some organizational overhauls that were being slow-walked for years were at long last prioritized and accelerated. Many of us experienced or saw the impact of the pandemic firsthand and developed a *What am I waiting for?* mentality about life and work.

My work and this book are shaped by my own experiences of realizing when it was time to rethink things and take action to reset and shape a next normal. These decisions became points of no return for me, from the moment in college I realized it was time to get serious about learning to the moment I decided to pursue a doctorate in psychology. That led me from teaching into private practice, during which time I discovered the nascent fields of executive coaching and leadership development consulting. Shaping a next normal that combined a therapy practice with executive coaching and leadership consulting opened into a leadership opportunity with a global consultancy. Those early consulting experiences enabled me to found my own leadership and organization development consulting firm, bringing together a community of coaches and consultants focused on change leadership.

I've been given so much on this journey. Those of you who have read my book *Ultra Leadership* already know that a huge transformation for me involved silencing my inner critics, getting up off the couch, becoming hooked on trail running, and eventually running a number of ultra-marathons. Each decision I've made to step into the work of rethinking and resetting different beliefs and behaviors has opened the door to a richer experience, a bigger next normal. That's the journey.

Throughout this book, you'll be asked to undertake a journey of your own—to rethink and reset how you approach your role as a leader, how you build and coach a high-performing team, and how you can lead change for your organization. To enable positive transformation for a team or an organization, we need to be on our own journey of positive personal transformation, an iterative process of learning and continuous improvement, which enables us to lead more intentionally and with greater impact.

Let me be clear: I don't see the process we'll explore in these pages as steps "to" more impactful leadership; I believe there are certain principles and practices we can adopt and tools we can apply as a way "of" leading that is more impactful.

This is the point of no return, the start line for a journey to create the next normal for you, your team, and your organization. It's time to "reach toward what is next." To begin, we'll explore the work of leading in the next normal. Let's get started.

CHAPTER 1

LEADING IN THE NEXT NORMAL

I USED TO HATE FOLLOWING A PROCESS. I thought of any process as a pair of handcuffs or a cage. If someone suggested I follow a process, I'd shrug it off, telling myself it was a bad process or it wouldn't work for me or, if I gave it a chance, something terrible would happen.

I was wrong. Hating process was an excuse for protecting my status quo. In reality, my "definitely not a process" mentality was indeed a process. And it was inefficient.

Early in my career, leading one of my first teams, I made talented and patient people suffer through my process for designing and preparing for the various workshops we would deliver. My process served *me* well: I could engage and disengage at will, work at my own pace, and still make my deadline. But it was frustrating and counterproductive for my team; I was killing engagement and disempowering people with my process.

As a leader, you own the experience you have and the results you deliver. That's accountability; it goes with the title and the salary. One of the main objectives of this book is to enable you to create a different experience for you, your team, and your organization. To do this, we should level-set and agree on some basics:

- Leadership

- Normal

- Next

- Rethink

- Reset

- Renew

LEADERSHIP

I've learned many lessons running ultra-marathons that are applicable to life in general and to leadership in particular. One of the most important lessons I've learned is that you can make a bigger impact by being more intentional about how you show up, what you focus on, and what you get done. Practice is the difference between an ugly 50K run and an enjoyable time on the trail.

Your task is always to keep getting better and working smarter. Every meeting you're in, every conversation you have, there is an opportunity to accept responsibility, to step in and create the next normal for yourself and others. What you say and do (or don't say and don't do) in those moments reflects whether or not you've decided to step into that leadership void.

Leadership is a choice. It takes courage. When you choose to lead, you are choosing to create something. When you choose to lead, you're disrupting the status quo. When you choose to lead, you're stepping into the unknown.

Managing is getting people to do things that are knowable. Leading gets people to join you in creating something different: a new experience, a bigger result, a next normal. Why don't more people step in? The simple answer is: an abundance of comfort and a scarcity of courage.

In *Leading Change*, business and management thought leader John Kotter writes, "Leadership creates organizations or adapts them to significantly changing circumstances. Leadership requires the will and skill to engage others and cause a positive outcome, defining what the future should look like, aligning people with the vision, and inspiring them to make it happen despite the obstacles." I like to boil things down even more: leaders enable positive transformation for their organization, their team, and the individuals they lead.

Leading in the next normal means *creating* the next normal. You are a creator, shaper, and leader of change. What will your organization need to look like and be capable of in order to create even more value in the next normal? What does each person need in order to shape their work and achieve their best results?

Leadership is a creative act that requires courage. Taking on the mantle of change leader and creating the next normal means you're signing up for all that goes with it. Leaders must be able to let go of what was, question what is, and reach toward what's next. It's challenging and rewarding work. It also requires you to be willing and able to step into uncertainty and work without a net.

Most people only step in to lead when they think they know the answer. You get promoted to the top of the organization because of what you know and what you're able to deliver. "I don't know" are words many senior leaders dread to speak. All the leaders in your organization today with titles like yours have the same opportunity and responsibility as you to create the next normal rather than accept it as it comes. Some will see what you see: both the opportunity and the responsibility. Some will see the opportunity and not feel or want the responsibility. For some, it will be the other way around: they'll feel responsible and not see the opportunity within that responsibility.

To lead only when you are certain you know the answer doesn't require a great deal of courage. These leaders aren't interested in creating the next normal; they're very concerned with protecting what they've got, maintaining the current state, and avoiding disruption and messiness. No one really likes disruption, and creativity is messy, but the best leaders are confident they can find the answer and are always willing to face down uncertainty and take the next step. That's what it takes to enable positive transformation and create the next normal.

NORMAL = CHANGE

When my kids were little, our family would watch an animated show called *Animaniacs*. One of the segments on the show featured two laboratory mice named Pinky and The Brain. At the start of each episode, Pinky would ask, "What are we going to do today, Brain?" Brain would answer, "The same thing we do every day, Pinky. Try and take over the world!" Pinky and The Brain had a normal—a routine that laid out what every day would be like.

Exploring what it means to shape and lead in a next normal requires a brief discussion of what "normal" means. "Next normal" presupposes a "last normal" or "this normal." What's "normal" anyway?

The pattern of recurring events we view as our current state, our status quo, is our "normal." It is our routine, our day-to-day experience of living and working. Our routine provides us with certainty and a sense of control over our environment. Changes to our routine disrupt our status quo. We don't like disruption or uncertainty because we perceive them as an intrusion into our pattern. Yet, if we were to pull back and view the pattern of our life through a telescope, we'd see that the disruptions are a part of the whole pattern.

When I was a therapist and a patient was feeling out of control, we would work on zooming out, pulling back their focus so they could see that this moment of disruption was not their whole life; it was just a *moment* in their life. That perspective would allow us to zoom back in and address the immediate with slightly less emotional charge. We'd focus on understanding and coping with moments like this so they would eventually occur less frequently over time.

The same process applies with leaders and teams feeling overwhelmed. We zoom out to see the disruption they've encountered, or are causing as a result of some unexpected or announced change, as part of a larger pattern. This helps them to focus on what they might do to enable their team or organization to navigate change and the related disruption more successfully.

Continuous change is normal. We don't like it, but the fact that things always change is part of the status quo. Our pattern isn't interrupted by change or disruption. The pattern is change, disruption, and iteration. Indeed, the more we see change as normative, the more we, our teams, and our organization will work to build the capability to shape and navigate continuous change.

NEXT = NEW TOOLS

The years 2020 and 2021 were a time of significant disruption for most organizations, teams, and people. There is no going back from the pandemic-induced changes to how we live and work.

Many organizations had to rapidly change how they drive value, go to market, engage their customers, streamline processes, and run their business. Smart leaders are seeing the present moment as a point of no return and an imperative to drive innovation and accelerate changes that will deliver a sustained competitive advantage. According to a McKinsey Survey of Global Executives published in October 2020, "The great acceleration in the use of technology, digitization, and new forms of working is going to be sustained. Many executives reported that they moved 20 to 25 times faster than they thought possible on things like building supply-chain redundancies, improving data security, and increasing the use of advanced technologies in operations."

How we live and work in every next normal will be different. The question we ask when faced with these changes is critical. Will we ask, *How do we go back? How will we survive?* or *What can we create to thrive in this moment?*

The question we ask indicates whether we are reacting to change or responding to it. It's an indicator of whether the oldest part of our brain and our emotions are driving our decisions or if we are engaging our higher-level brain functions to ensure a measured and productive response. If you've been called to leadership, being reactive is the most counterproductive tendency. Your organization and the team you lead need you to be able to respond. As we gain our footing in this next normal, will you be the pilot or a passenger?

Like first responders rushing toward danger, as a leader, your responsibility is to aim for and take on challenges. The question is never, *Why is this happening to me?* None of us are immune to the randomness of life. No one promised us a rose garden. The question for leaders is always, *So, now what?*

Anyone can be a disruptor. As a leader, you need to be a *positive* disruptor and enable *positive* transformation. This begins with your awareness that the changes you are responding to or causing will be experienced as a disruption to people's status quo. You'll be messing with someone's comfort zone, "harshing someone's mellow." How will you keep people engaged while they're experiencing the instinctual reactivity and emotions that go along with feeling disrupted? How will you help your people see disruption as necessary and positive? How do you bring others to your point of view that going back or maintaining the status quo are no longer viable options? How do you help people want to change?

Leading in the next normal really means creating the next normal. This is a moment for rethinking how we show up and lead; for resetting our teams to perform within a new paradigm, to shape and navigate through change; and for renewing our organizations in the process.

Here's the catch: creating your next normal begins with enabling your own positive transformation. I used to design and deliver well-received and highly-rated leadership development programs based on the belief that learning and development don't miraculously occur as a result of how awesome a workshop or the content may be. The process is far more important than the content. Real success depends on each individual engaging with the process and deciding to do the work as a willing and intentional participant.

I have coached numerous leaders at different points in their careers, many who were stepping up a level into a new role, taking on a new team or major initiative, or leading a larger part of their organization or even the whole organization. What they share in common with every other leader is that succeeding at that next step proves to be more challenging. Each learned they could not lead higher-level teams with more complex responsibilities in the same way they led their previous teams.

Many leaders learn this lesson the hard way. They step up and immediately begin doing what worked in the prior role. They reach into their mental hard drive, their memory, and use what worked last time. And it doesn't work as well. They learn that this new role with a new team will require updating their approach. They're forced to rethink how they show up and achieve the level of success they're used to. What will they focus on? How will they bring this team together, and for what purpose? How will they create alignment? How will they bring out the best in their direct reports? How will they ensure all the plates keep spinning? They have to shift their mindset, develop new skills, and leverage a new tool set in order to succeed in their new role.

The work begins when we open ourselves to the possibility that we don't know everything, and there may be a way to approach our work that makes it feel easier, where we expend less energy and achieve the same or better results. This is a moment for rethinking how we see the work of leadership and how we show up to do that work. It is a moment for resetting how we lead teams and renewing how our organizations navigate through change.

RETHINK

Many leaders have a tendency to chase shiny objects; I've been guilty of it myself. One leader I coached knew he chased shiny objects, even though he knew it was counterproductive. It drove his team crazy. When I asked him to think about what he got out of it, he said, "I don't get anything out of it." I said, "That's not true. If you didn't get anything out of it, you'd have stopped doing it by now. Go think about it."

At our next call, I asked him again, "What do you think you get out of chasing shiny objects all the time?" He said it was a way to protect himself from any perception that he wasn't driving value. He needed to be the one who saw the next great thing and brought others along. While at one point the behavior may have produced positive results, it had become a hindrance to his ability to lead effectively. The realization opened the possibility for his next positive transformation.

Creating your next normal will require you to rethink things and reset what you believe about team building and leadership, management and governance, and organizational change and renewal. In fact, I encourage you to grab a journal or pad as you read this book so you can pause from time to time and record your observations and answers to some of the questions included.

The first part of rethinking something is to become clear about what we think about it at present. We can ask ourselves, *What principles drive my approach to leadership? or What behaviors and practices are critical to my being the most effective leader?* Bringing our current beliefs into focus sets the table for rethinking what we believe and becoming more intentional in how we speak and act as we go about our work as leaders.

All behavior has meaning; we only do things that we believe deliver something of value for us. Certain behaviors protect us from external forces while others expand our control over external forces.

Whenever we stop and think about the principles we adhere to as leaders, we're able to reflect on the efficacy of those principles and the impact each one has on our behavior.

In his terrific book, *Think Again*, organizational psychologist and author Adam Grant writes, "We live in a rapidly changing world, where we need to spend as much time rethinking as we do thinking." He suggests we think more like scientists, who engage with contrary points of view to weigh the reliability and validity of our hypotheses. Of course, we can only do that if we're willing to be wrong from time to time.

Grant's suggestion highlights the value in seeing rethinking as a two-part process. Reflecting is the first part. We have to look honestly at what we believe about leadership and how those beliefs are impacting our behavior as leaders. Does the way we think about leadership and management actually produce the positive experience and results we want?

The second part of rethinking is dialogue. Solitary reflection only gets us so far. Conversation with a trusted friend, colleague, mentor, or coach can yield beautiful fruit. Dialogue with another human being about what we're thinking, feeling, or considering builds on and enhances our reflection. We need to submit our work to peer review.

Rethinking how you show up to lead is a big ask. You've accumulated lots of behaviors and practices throughout your career that have become the habits that shape how you approach your work. Some still work; others may have become counterproductive. The reality is that creating your next normal as a leader will likely require more subtraction than addition. Most likely, you won't need to learn something new—you'll need to unlearn something that no longer serves you. That will require a choice: maintain the status quo or take action to shift your mindset and create your very own next normal.

RESET

How are the principles you hold working for you? How effective and productive are the behaviors and practices you use to do your work?

Resetting is hard work. Wanting to change and actually putting in the work it takes to change are two different things. Our aspiration to change runs headlong into an inner and equally strong commitment to not change. Organizational psychologists and researchers Robert Kegan and Lisa Laskow Lahey call this paradox "competing commitments." The competing commitments within us manifest as self-limiting or self-generated barriers to change.

The status quo holds a tremendous amount of sway over us. A study published in the *Journal of the American Medical Association* in 2013 found that one in four men won't change their lifestyle by eating better, exercising, or quitting smoking after a heart attack, stroke, or other major cardiac event. At a meeting of the Global Medical Forum in 2004, Dr. Edward Miller, Dean of the Medical Faculty at Johns Hopkins University and CEO of Johns Hopkins Medicine from 1997 to 2012, placed the percentage much higher. The research indicated, "If you look at people after coronary-artery bypass grafting, two years later, 90 percent of them have not changed their lifestyle." Miller said, "And that's been studied over and over and over again. And so, we're missing some link in there. Even though they know they have a very bad disease, and they know they should change their lifestyle, for whatever reason, they can't."

Competing commitments are real. And as we age, we become more set in our ways. We generate routines, rituals, and behaviors that have become our normal. Our normal is our comfort zone. To break out of our comfort zone, we have to go to the edge and push farther.

When it comes to resetting how we show up and how we lead, we have our work cut out for us. While there are some similarities, each person's process to reset is different. When I'm coaching leaders who've made a commitment to reset a particular behavior, I ask them how they've committed to and followed through with changing something in the past. What worked to keep them accountable? What didn't?

Let's look at a real example of a leader rethinking and resetting a particular behavior. Kelly is a senior leader in the finance organization at her company. She has a reputation for being intelligent, capable, and responsible. She gets stuff done. She also tends toward introversion, so in larger meetings, she would respond to specific questions but otherwise keep quiet. This was especially true in cross-functional settings.

Our conversations about this behavior revealed that this was a self-protective act. Earlier in her career, Kelly worked at an organization where more junior people learned "not to speak unless spoken to." While her current behavior worked at one time, it was becoming counterproductive now. In a 360-process, we learned her behavior was leading others to think she had nothing to add or question why was she even at the meetings.

We set a plan to reset how she shows up and engages in meetings in a way that suited her leadership style. First, she made a conscious decision to be seen as creating value in the conversations she is present for, instead of just being available to answer questions if needed. Knowing this would take practice, she enrolled a trusted colleague to watch her and grade her in different meetings each week. They would meet for fifteen minutes each Friday to discuss her progress. She also put a note in front of her at each meeting that read: "Don't just sit there, say something."

Aware that some of her peers like talking just to hear themselves talk, Kelly was adamant she didn't want to behave similarly. She wanted to expand or deepen the conversations, not just get noticed. We devised to look for insertion points where she could interject and make her presence known in a productive way. This helped her to be a positive disruptor, not just a disrupter.

Kelly began practicing speaking up earlier in meetings, using a simple, three-step technique. When she saw her opening, she'd say, "Here's what I hear you saying," and paraphrase the last comment. Then she'd say, "Here's what you've got me thinking," and elaborate a bit. Then, she'd move the conversation forward by saying, "Here's my question." The technique elicited positive feedback from her colleagues. She was now thought of as someone who was really listening, who asked amazing questions, and who kept things moving.

By rethinking and resetting how she showed up as a leader, Kelly created a next normal for herself and the people she was engaging with. Her reflection, dialogue, and practice led to renewal.

RENEW

The process of resetting and renewing involves recognizing the patterns of how we think and act so we can put in place mechanisms to disrupt the patterns we want to change. This process helps us develop a new default setting—a fresh, revitalized, iterated, and transformed way of showing up and leading.

The work of rethinking and resetting results in an experience of renewal. This renewal takes form as our next normal. I've worked with many leaders over the years who, like Kelly, decided it was time to rethink and reset in order to have a different experience and achieve different results. Their decision to answer in the affirmative that voice asking, "Will I lead today?" begins the journey that results in significant business transformation and life-changing personal and professional transformations as well.

Our brains move pretty fast. Gerald Zaltman's research indicating that 95 percent of our purchase decision-making occurs in our subconscious minds is widely accepted in the field of marketing. C. S. Soon and other researchers have shown that our brains are already aware of a decision before we make it. It's a good bet that, after years working as a leader in an organization, your decision-making might have become automatic. You're going to have to make a sustained, conscious effort to begin the journey and see it through. If we're going to transform ourselves, our teams, and our organizations, there's no other way. You've probably done this before in some shape or form. Now, you just need to remember and connect with that muscle memory.

In your work, you have probably experienced many ups and downs and twists and turns. Before we move on, recall some of your prior experiences of change:

- Do a quick mental review of the many initiatives/moments where you joined others to create positive change.

- Reflect on one moment or initiative that stands out as something of a high point—a time when you felt most alive, effective, or proud of your involvement.

- What made it a high-point experience? What happened? When was it? What was the experience like?

- What did you learn from the experience that is important to remember and apply now?

One leader I coached, Terry, was tapped as CEO of her organization. She took on the role at a time when growth had flattened. She needed to implement a number of changes to increase revenue and recapture market share.

We walked through the previous questions, and she reminded herself of a number of different instances of navigating change she had experienced. One that stood out was when her team's leader was available and transparent when explaining what was changing, why things were changing, how the changes would be implemented, and what the impact would be on the team and each person. The way Terry's leader created a container for the team to process what was occurring enabled them to more fully participate in shaping the next normal for their organization.

Terry wanted to emulate that leader and do everything in her power to create an environment for her team to get better at navigating change and leading others through it. After she committed to that goal, she was able to see real progress within a year's time. The organization was experiencing growth again, and the disruption to engagement was minimal.

Creating our next normal requires us to evaluate and intentionally disrupt the status quo. The following chapters provide ideas for rethinking, resetting, and renewing what we believe about leadership, management, and change so we can successfully drive positive transformation.

CHAPTER 2

DRIVING CHANGE

LET'S START WITH TWO TRUE STORIES. First, a guy, let's call him Bill, joined a large public company as CIO. In his second week, Bill announced, via email, that in two weeks' time, no one would be allowed to work on a Mac. They would be a 100 percent Windows environment. One small problem: the company his organization had purchased just before his arrival—a company with over 3,000 employees—was a 100 percent Apple iOS environment.

Another true story. A COO, let's call him Ted, decided his company would run more efficiently by reorganizing. No reason given. Ted drafted a new organizational chart and emailed it to his team, writing, "This is our new reporting structure. Inform your teams."

Don't be like Bill and Ted. They introduced sweeping change without the necessary time or big-picture attention required to create positive disruption. They did not take their companies on an excellent adventure.

Change is an intentionally disruptive act, and leaders can enable their organizations, teams, and people to better handle those disruptions. All leadership is essentially change leadership. Leaders are responsible for guiding the organization from its current state to its future state, painting a picture of the future. Leaders are responsible for engaging people and encouraging teamwork to realize that future. Leaders are responsible for creating the conditions for people to continually expand their capacity to contribute. All of this work causes disruption and, if done right, enables positive transformation, enhancing your organization's competitive advantage in an ever-changing environment.

Leading smarter change efforts to shape the next normal requires a balanced approach to change, transition, and empowerment.

CHANGE

Way back in 1991, Richard Beatty and David Ulrich authored an article entitled, "Re-energizing the Mature Organization." They wrote, "The challenge for a mature organization—which has based its success on security and stability—is to meet a changing environment, and to respond to changes in a manner that will revitalize its structure and competitive edge." While Beatty and Ulrich looked at change in mature organizations, the model is relevant to our conversation about leading change in any organization. If we're going to lead change and shape the next normal, we're going to have to think bigger and widen our focus.

Beatty and Ulrich developed this graphic to illustrate what requires the attention of leadership over time to create lasting change.

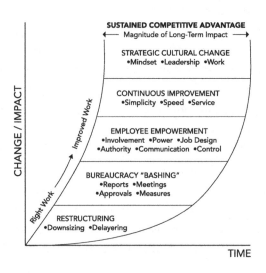

Beatty and Ulrich's model is a powerful reminder of the scope and nature of organizational change. What they described as a "mature" organization in 1991 is almost any organization today, not just one that's been around a long time. Every change initiative is undertaken in order to minimize some risk, reduce some expense, or generate more revenue with the hope that these things enable the organization to maintain or gain some sustained competitive advantage. Sustained competitive advantage takes time and a wider focus. The Bill and Ted approach won't get you there.

Beatty and Ulrich illustrate the true scope of organizational change. When you initiate change for your organization, you are promising the future state you are describing will be better than the current state. Despite considerable effort and expense, multiple studies of organizational change continue to demonstrate that 70 percent of leaders are making promises that they can't keep. One reason is their focus is too narrow, usually limited to change management on process and structure. It's never as simple as making some change to the organizational structure or operating model.

While changes to structure can be announced and implemented fairly quickly, taken alone, the effectiveness of those changes is limited because of the powerful hold the current normal has on people. The existing paradigm is, in many cases, a bureaucracy designed to ease anxiety for those at the top of the organization by ensuring things happen in an efficient and cost-effective manner; people spend an inordinate amount of time, energy, and resources reporting status up to senior leadership. Reorganizing organizational structure without rethinking and resetting how work flows throughout the structure can stall any change initiative. Changes to structure and process are external in nature. You decide. You announce. You execute. Your people react. You can't stop there.

To get to real sustained competitive advantage, you'll have to encourage internal changes in how people and teams think, engage, and contribute. That's more complicated and takes more time. It's messier and more difficult work to help people, teams, and the whole organization go through a simultaneously individual and collective experience of rethinking, resetting, and renewing in order to participate in shaping the next normal. Leadership doesn't change people; leadership gets people to want to change.

The challenge for leadership when initiating any change is to empower people to stay as engaged, available, productive, and accountable as possible while the changes are being introduced and implemented. The work of leadership is to create the conditions where people choose to stay engaged and navigate through transformation.

I've heard many leaders talk about a major change they had in mind for the organization, a shift in either how the organization creates value or how the business operates or both, in order to maintain or enhance competitive advantage. Someone will say, "We'll have to do some change management there." What the heck does that mean? I find it means something different for every leader who utters those words. In many cases, it means a video message or email from the CEO, a lot of work by HR and Finance to ensure everything lines up, and perhaps some training in a new process. That's the Bill and Ted approach.

When you begin to shape the next normal, you're setting a marker. You're announcing that something, or perhaps everything, will be different from this moment on. Your announcement has an impact. We experience change as an external event, something we learn about and that happens "to us." In this sense, we experience change as a disruption of our normal circumstances and our status quo. In these moments, we can feel less certain and less in control of our situation. To succeed in delivering on your promise of organizational transformation and the creation of a next normal, you'll need to widen your focus and think differently. Changing an organization requires people to change, and we can't change people—we can only help them *want* to change.

TRANSITION

Preeminent thought leader William Bridges called the human process of navigating change a *transition*. While change is an external event, an alteration in circumstances that we face and exist in, transition is the psychological process we go through in accepting and working through that change. According to Bridges, transitions have three phases: Ending, Losing, Letting Go; the Neutral Zone; and the New Beginning. Once we are presented with a change event, we move through the three phases on the way to full acceptance and participation in change.

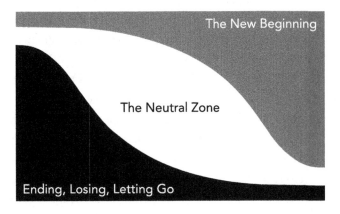

CREDIT: WILLIAM BRIDGES

Every transition begins with an ending and an experience of loss or letting go of a familiar process or routine, such as one's reporting structure. The Neutral Zone is an in-between space where the announced change is not yet fully realized, the gap between the old reality and the new one. The New Beginning is when the changes are fully accepted, adopted, applied, and realized.

Moving through the Neutral Zone, we may experience chaos, confusion, doubt, and discomfort. The Neutral Zone is where we may rethink and reset our expectations, behaviors, and practices. We experiment with new ways of working and being, and we establish new networks and relationships, navigating through the uncertainty of letting go and into a new way of engaging and working.

We would love to skip the Neutral Zone or try to race through it, but going through all three phases is unavoidable, and everyone has their own pace. There's no avoiding the Neutral Zone. And because there may be many changes happening at once, we may find ourselves working through several transitions at once. Taking a balanced approach to leading change means helping people through their experience of transition—including the Neutral Zone—so they can remain as engaged and productive as possible as your team or organization navigates through change.

Everyone reacts or responds to change differently, meaning that everyone's transition through the three phases will be different as well. Bridges describes this as the "marathon effect." Everyone is lined up in the shoot waiting for the race to begin. When the starter's pistol fires, there are runners in the front who take off fast. Many get caught in the crowd, and their start is a shuffle while they find their path and opportunity to break out of the pack. Some decide they're going to walk the whole way. Some don't even show up for the race.

Everyone reacts to announced change at a different point, with different emotions underlying their decisions about how to participate or not. Some people may fully accept announced changes and enthusiastically participate in making it real across the organization. It doesn't mean they skipped to the New Beginning phase; it just means their internal process was quicker.

How fast and how well someone moves through a transition can depend on a lot of things. It can depend on the scope of change and how much it disrupts our status quo. It can depend on our ability to handle uncertainty and actively rethink and reset how we approach our work. Mostly, how people transition depends on how the change is announced and how the change journey is managed by leadership. How are you encouraging people to want to undertake the change journey with you?

There's much leadership can do to help people transition and fully engage to make the New Beginning a reality. As people focus on what's ending and what they may be losing as a result of change, they may feel insecure, anxious, sad, uncertain, fearful, helpless, or angry. Sometimes when we encounter intense emotions, we want to shut the conversation down because it makes us uncomfortable. Our ability to help our teams and our people at this point depends on our capacity for empathy. Our responsibility is to meet people with understanding and compassion to help them fully process the change, stay engaged, and reshape their work in order to participate in a productive way.

When you are actively leading a significant change, consider the best way to convene a conversation about change and transition with your team and with each person. When talking about change, be as clear and detailed as possible about what's changing and why, how the changes will be implemented, and how you imagine the changes will impact the team and each person. If you don't know, say you don't know and that you'll do what you can to find out.

When it's clear that someone is not understanding or embracing change, be curious. Their "no" might really mean, "I'm afraid." We don't like to admit when we're afraid, so it comes out as resistance to change. This is when you have to lean into conversations that may make you uncomfortable. Invite people to identify real or perceived losses. Who might lose something? What do they think they are going to lose? How do they feel about those losses?

Remember, subjective and emotional losses are as real as any other losses. Every change will cause other changes. Ask the team or person if they see any unintended consequences for them. Ask them to shift and consider the positive aspects of the change. Don't try to sell them on it. Ask them to share what they think will be gained as a result of the change. What could be in it for the team and for each person?

While people are in the Neutral Zone, they may also be experiencing confusion and uncertainty as they try to work in a different way. The rules may be changing; they may be expected to learn new processes and engage with new people. They may feel less confident about how to contribute as things change. They may feel impatient with the pace of change or with the perceived progress of others.

During this phase, be on the lookout for signs people feel resentful about how the change is impacting things. Listen for statements indicating people are resistant or cynical about the change initiative or anxious about their role as the organization changes. Your ability to stay present and engaged and listen empathically is vitally important.

Taking a balanced approach means accepting that other people aren't distracting you from your work. Helping other people through their transition *is* your work. Let people know their feelings are legitimate, and it's okay to feel uncertain or a bit lost. The Neutral Zone can be like a fog for some people. Our job is to find people where they are and help guide them out of the fog.

Set more frequent meetings with people, according to an agreed cadence, to check-in and provide feedback on how they're making their way through the Neutral Zone. Remind them of what's in their control. Remind them of the team's shared goals. Agree on short-term wins specific to the team's shared goals and the change underway. Celebrate wins as much as possible.

Indicators that a person has made their way through the Neutral Zone include increased energy and productivity, an eagerness to keep learning, renewed openness, and a return of confidence. As you notice people completing their transition to the New Beginning, make note of it. Remember and celebrate the change and transition journey they've made. Reinforce the behaviors that contributed to their success.

Remember, each person is going to make their way through the change and transition process in their own way and in their own time. There's no one-size-fits-all answer. We have to stay connected and curious in order to help each person navigate through change and transition in their particular way. Impatience may make us want to push or pull people along. We need to fight that urge. Our work is to engage with empathy and help people navigate through the change journey.

Navigating change involves finding the answers to some key questions: What's changing? Why are we changing? How are these changes going to be executed? How do these changes impact my team and me? What's the benefit to me? What happens if we don't change? The more people we help make their way through their individual transitions, the greater the likelihood we will build a change-worthy organization.

EMPOWERMENT

A ship is seaworthy if it is safe and fit to undertake a sea voyage and weather a variety of conditions. Like seaworthy ships, we need our organizations to be change-worthy—able to learn, adapt, and act quickly in an always-changing and sometimes volatile marketplace. There will always be another change because change isn't a bug in the system; it's a feature. Your work is to empower your team to be exceptional at navigating and leading transformation, thereby building an unsinkable organization.

Transformative leadership empowers people by focusing on both driving business results in support of change and developing people by helping them manage their transitions. When we are out of balance, we may drive results while losing people through disengagement or departure; conversely, we may make everyone feel great and fail to achieve stated business objectives. To empower people and build a change-worthy, unsinkable organization, you need to remember your ABCs:

- **ALIGN PEOPLE**—Create a clear direction (vision, mission, strategy) and a plan (structure, roles and responsibilities, systems, processes) to make change real.

- **BUILD BENCH STRENGTH (CAPACITY)**—Build leadership
  and organizational capacity while creating a state of
  "change-worthiness."

- **COORDINATE ACTION**—Ensure ongoing follow-up and
  follow-through with tracking and adjustment mechanisms
  to lead and manage through the change.

My colleague Pat Newmann and I created a checklist for leaders
to help them shape and execute a successful transformation strategy
and plan. Whenever you're at the front edge of organizational transformation, take a look at the following list of items. Read each statement carefully. Is this something that you will require for your change
initiative to succeed? If so, is it completed, in progress, or missing?

Look at the items you determine are needed for your change initiative to succeed. For each item, is the work: done and working? in
progress and needs some work? or missing and needs to be started?
If, by your estimation, more than one-third of the items are still in
progress or missing, your organization may not be "change-worthy"
yet. There is still work to do.

The checklist uses the pronoun "we." Take this to mean the leaders responsible for the change initiative, as well as key stakeholders.

ALIGN PEOPLE:

- We have an executive sponsor willing and able to build a
  leadership coalition for change (is that you?).

- We know and understand how the senior leadership team
  will work to lead the entire effort.

- We know and understand the organizational vision (two to
  three years out).

- We know and understand the purpose for this change
  initiative (why are we changing?).

- We know and understand what the impact will be if this change initiative is not successful.

- We know and understand how the project management of the change initiative will be conducted and by whom.

- We know and understand the key milestones and timelines for this change initiative.

- We know and understand the success measures for the change initiative.

- We know and understand what every employee and leader can do to help this succeed.

- We know and understand who will provide leadership for various elements of the change initiative, including who makes what decisions.

- We know and understand how this change initiative will impact the whole value chain (activities performed to bring our product/service to market).

- We know and understand how this change initiative will impact other key partners inside of the organization.

- We have allocated adequate resources (e.g., people, time, money, consulting) to support the change initiative.

BUILD BENCH STRENGTH (CAPACITY):

- We understand and accept that change is normal and ongoing.

- We have a plan for engaging employees throughout the change process, so they continue to learn and grow as they take part in making the change work.

- We are willing and able to adjust plans and approaches to implementing the change as conditions require.

- We have the talent (people, skills, and practices) at all levels key to leading the change initiative.

- There is a shared commitment to continuous learning among those responsible for leading and managing the change.

- We have the strong and demonstrated engagement of middle managers who are committed to making this change happen.

- We have a clear picture of the leadership mindset and skills we will need to lead change successfully.

- We have the capacity to assess and develop the leadership mindset and skills we will need to lead change successfully.

- We have an outplacement plan, if necessary.

- We have retention plans for keeping the people and skills we do not want to lose.

- We have a talent management/workforce development strategy and plan that assures the timely development of mission-critical people and skills.

- We have appropriate engagement of external vendors and suppliers in the value chain and their commitment to making this change happen.

- We have appropriate engagement of internal key partners and stakeholders and their commitment to making this change happen.

- We have a commitment to institutionalizing change, so there is no turning back.

- We have the skills to create the policies and procedures to ensure we will institutionalize the change.

- We have a culture that will encourage experimentation and learning throughout the change initiative.

- We have a culture of mutual trust and cooperation that will enable us to leverage differences to produce best thinking.

COORDINATE ACTION:

- We have a strong leadership team that oversees the change initiative and stays engaged.

- Regular meetings are scheduled for the change leadership team to track progress and resolve issues.

- We have an agreed decision-making model that enables the change leadership team to resolve issues.

- We have a communications plan that is being followed and features success stories.

- We have a mechanism in place for providing regular and ongoing feedback about how the change is progressing.

- We have a change roadmap to provide ongoing visibility into key success indicators.

- We have a clearly defined and trackable work breakdown structure.

- We design and implement policies and guidelines that support the changes to be made.

- We have an identified project management team guiding the workflow and ensuring progress according to timeline and budget.

- We have planned and scheduled activities designed to honor the past and enable employees to engage with change and let go of how it used to be.

- We track and address perceived loss and individual and organization unit-level resistance to change.

- We have built-in celebrations that will acknowledge achievements of key milestones.

- We have a plan for rewarding follow-up and follow-through.

Using the checklist as a starting point for designing your change strategy and plan ensures you will take a balanced approach to leading transformation, focusing attention on changing structure or systems and processes while also enabling people to stay engaged and develop individual and collective capacity to fully participate in a new way. This balanced approach is critical because organizational change relies on individual change.

When people transition and adapt to change, they develop a new mindset that manifests as new behaviors and practices. That takes time. It's not as easy as either Bill or Ted imagined. When enough people come to understand, accept, and decide to participate in change, the organization changes, too.

As you begin to shape the next normal, remembering your ABCs will help you build a team and an organization that navigates change well. Remember that understanding how people transition in response to change is an important part of the work of transformative leadership.

In the next chapter, we'll look at the organizing principles that have shaped our prior "normals" and those principles that are increasingly shaping the next normal we are experiencing to varying degrees in our organizations today. Becoming clearer about the principles that shape the point of view we bring to the work of leadership, management, and change can enable us to bring our next normal into greater focus.

CHAPTER 3

THE GOSPEL ACCORDING TO YOU
(YOUR LEADERSHIP POV)

IN MY COLLEGIATE WORLD RELIGIONS CLASS, we learned that religions are how people grapple with and answer life's ultimate questions. Different religions have different answers to such questions as: How did the world begin? What are we supposed to do with human existence? How are we supposed to treat other humans and the planet? What happens after this life? Christians, Jews, Muslims, Hindus, Buddhists, and every other religious group have their own answers to these questions. Each religion's answers become the organizing principles for their adherents.

As long as our religion's answers satisfy our questions, we remain practitioners of our particular religion; we follow that "gospel." When the answers don't fully satisfy our curiosity, or when we come into contact with another religion's answers, we may rethink our relationship with one religion, align with the answers that better address our questions, and revise our organizing principles. We don't have to just accept the answers others provide, and questioning the answers is not a bad thing. In fact, for leaders, it is crucial.

Leaders have the power to replicate and scale what they believe in order to impact the decisions and actions of hundreds or thousands of people. Believe me, your team knows your point of view (POV) and can cite the "gospel according to you" quite well. They repeat it with their teams and spread the word far and wide. The organizing principles you hold create a paradigm in which countless decisions are made about structure, process, culture, and capabilities.

The disruptions of 2020-21 accelerated the need to rethink and reset some of the principles that inform how we approach leadership, management, and change. But even if we hadn't traversed a point of no return caused by a global pandemic, it is always a good thing to periodically revisit the assumptions upon which many of our leadership and business decisions rest.

Because we may change our answers, our gospel must be subject to constant rethinking, resetting, and renewing.

RETHINKING

Each of us gets to come up with our own set of answers to life's ultimate questions, our own gospel. We even have our own gospel about life's not-so-ultimate questions: real Christmas tree or artificial? Star Wars or Star Trek? Tastes Great or Less Filling?

You have a point of view about market trends and the opportunities and risks to your business. You have a point of view about how your organization can create more value and what your organization should do to maintain a competitive advantage. You have certain beliefs about what organizations are and how they should run, and what high-performing teams look like and do to succeed. You have a point of view about how the people who report to you need to behave and deliver. You may hold strong opinions about change and how organizations need to manage it.

At work, we are driven by our belief system, the operating principles guiding our decisions and actions. If, like Gordon Gekko in Oliver Stone's film *Wall Street*, we believe that "Greed, for lack of a better word, is good," we might behave in ways consistent with how that character behaved. If, like a multitude of business school alumni, we believe Milton Friedman was right, we might make decisions about driving revenue and managing expenses and risk in order to maximize returns for stakeholders. If we believe organizations are machines, then we might work to make our machine run as efficiently as possible.

Our beliefs and behaviors become automatic and even unconscious; we develop an "auto-pilot." We become set in our ways. Habits form. The English poet John Dryden said, "We first make our habits. Then our habits make us." We begin and end our days with particular rituals. The key to our development is to intentionally rethink and reset the pattern in order to renew our experience.

Every now and then, we need to ask, *Why do I do it this way? What do I get out of this? Is there a better way?* The journey starts when we engage in conscious and intentional self-reflection.

What you think and what you say and do (or don't say and don't do) every day reverberates through your team and across the organization, shaping what people do and how they work. The ground upon which all this activity occurs is the foundation provided by your organizing principles.

You might say this book is a record of my most current answers to these questions about management, leadership, and change. Here are the organizing principles I see as foundational to being a successful leader in the next normal:

- The Organization Is a Living System

- Change Is Normative

- Leading Is a Balancing Act

- Build Bridges, Not Walls

- You're a Coach, Not a Machine Operator

- To Win Is to Learn and Serve

THE ORGANIZATION IS A LIVING SYSTEM

The purpose of a machine is unchanging: it's meant to produce a certain product or effect. Each part of the machine has a function, and it makes sense to want that machine to run as smoothly and efficiently as possible. For over one hundred years, we've talked about the organization as a machine. It's time we stopped. Continued use of the machine analogy when talking about organizations is a problem. Organizations are entities comprised of people with a shared purpose, and in this sense, they are living systems. Every individual in the organization is their own living system, and each team is its own system.

Living systems are complex and adaptive. Living systems strive for equilibrium. Living systems exist as a whole; no part can survive or thrive while another dies or languishes. Living systems are self-renewing and expansive.

CHANGE IS NORMATIVE

Living things change. Everything that is alive develops, learns, and adapts, including each individual, team, and organization. It's happening now, and it'll happen again.

We forget or try to forget that change isn't a disruption in our pattern, it's part of the pattern. It's not a bug in the system; it's a feature. We've known this and bemoaned this reality since before the Greek philosopher Heraclitus said, "Change is the only constant in life."

Knowing change is a constant impacts how people see the organization and how tightly they hold onto their status quo. When we accept that change is normative, we stop resisting it and begin building an organization that is good at change. To succeed in business, you need an organization that is change-worthy—able to learn, adapt, and act quickly in an always-changing and sometimes volatile marketplace.

LEADING IS A BALANCING ACT

At an organizational level, balancing involves combining business outcomes with cultural and people goals. Organizations and teams with a results-only focus tend to experience more churn and retention issues. Organizations on the other end of the spectrum may be cool places to work where everyone enjoys one another and likes being there, but not a lot gets done.

At a team level, taking a balanced approach means dedicating time and attention to dynamics that impact collective and individual performance. At an individual level, it means placing as much importance on developing "human skills" (e.g., openness, expression, communication, empathy) as on "hard skills" (e.g., knowledge and job-specific techniques).

The best leaders drive to achieve agreed upon business outcomes. They also have a relentless and equally strong focus on culture and people. They know that even if they aren't responsible for every element of the work, they are ultimately accountable for not just driving business results but also for creating an environment where people feel like they matter, can shape their work, and achieve their best results.

BUILD BRIDGES, NOT WALLS

Some organizations are hampered by hierarchical structures and artificial, self-imposed boundaries with multiple, sometimes incompatible, processes that make it harder for employees to engage, collaborate, and execute. These organizations may still be stuck in the "organization-as-machine" mindset.

Remaining overly siloed doesn't help you decrease expenses or increase revenue—quite the contrary. Siloes slow the flow of information, impede decision-making, and hinder smooth execution, all of which manifest as increased risk.

The complexity and pace of business today require shorter cycle times for making and acting on critical decisions. Removing artificial and self-imposed boundaries allows information to flow more easily between teams and across functions and geographies. While it's hard work, collaboration pays off for organizations, employees, and customers.

YOU'RE A COACH, NOT A MACHINE OPERATOR

If the organization is a machine, your role as a manager is to keep it running efficiently. Employees are simply cogs in the machine, meaning you tell them what to do and direct them on how to do it. Such an approach may be faster and easier for you, but in the long run, it's a counterproductive pattern.

If, on the other hand, you see the organization as a living system, change as normative, balance as healthy, and collaboration as imperative, then your role is not to tend to the machine. Your role as a leader is to enable positive transformation for the organization, the team, and the people you lead.

Leadership that relies on position or title is prevalent in a hierarchical, fixed, organization-as-machine institution. In a living system, the work of leadership is to create the conditions where people say "yes" when asked to engage and contribute. That's a "coach approach."

Coaching is closely related to educating: we are drawing the answers out of our people and pointing them in the right direction. We see the organization as a living system and the people within it as living systems capable of learning, growing, and contributing more value to the whole.

TO WIN IS TO LEARN AND SERVE

If you've come up through the ranks in a hierarchical, siloed organization, you may be operating with the organizing principle that tells you to win is to know more than anyone else. Your deep experience and expertise are how you added value. They're what got you recognized. The pressure to maintain your status in this type of organization is enormous.

In these organizations, to not know something is to lose. As a result, leaders spend most of their time protecting their silo and maneuvering against one another for favor and resources. Information is fed up to a few at the top of the organizational chart to ease unending anxiety. That's not an efficient machine, and it's certainly not a healthy living system.

Winning isn't knowing more than others. Because you're working in a constantly changing environment, certainty is something you can't count on. Winning is embracing uncertainty, learning faster, and sharing knowledge in service of the organization, your team, and others.

RESETTING AND RENEWING

Leaders have much to be concerned about. A lot is riding on the decisions you make. Two of the ultimate questions organizations must answer are: how are we driving value? and how are we running our business? How we answer them raises more questions about how we lead people and manage tasks along the way.

Smart senior leaders are always rethinking how best to move the organization from Point A to Point B. To succeed, you need to enable groups of people to work together as high-performing teams. You have to figure out how to help people develop themselves and raise their performance from good to better. To take on all this work, you must strive to keep yourself on a path of continuous improvement and conscious leadership.

Hopefully, this chapter is sparking a rethinking and resetting of your leadership POV, your gospel. I listed six organizing principles that reflect my POV on the nature of organizations, change, and leadership. What do you think? Do you agree or disagree? If you disagree, what's your position? What assumptions inform your POV? How does your POV impact the decisions you make as a leader? This is another good place to break out the journal to rethink and reconfirm or rewrite your organizing principles. Let's use mine as a template:

- Organizations are Living Systems.
  - I think organizations are...
  - Organizations are successful when they...
- Change is Normative
  - Organizational change is...
  - People resist change because...
  - My role in leading change is to...
- Leading is a Balancing Act
  - Leadership is...
  - The difference between management and leadership is...
- Build Bridges, Not Walls
  - If we relied more/less on hierarchy, it would produce...
  - Authority flows from...
- You're a Coach, Not a Machine Operator
  - A team is...
  - As a team leader, it's my job to...
- To Win is to Learn and Serve
  - I define winning as...
  - When it comes to leadership, the three things I value most are... (e.g., honesty, loyalty, creativity, flexibility, etc.)

Perhaps how you completed some of these prompts has changed since the last time you reflected on your leadership point of view. Maybe not. The point is to revisit the questions from time to time and remind yourself what drives your leadership point of view. Your answer to each prompt depends on the assumptions you make. Each answer has implications for how you show up and the style you employ as a leader.

Reflect on your last month. Did you spend a lot of time telling people what to do? Was your focus on efficiency or productivity? Did you act to protect your status quo or demonstrate an openness to change? Did you actively work across team or functional boundaries or out-maneuver others? Did you take time to coach your team or solve their problems for them? When you place your answers to the prompts next to your reflection on how you've led in the past month, how congruent are your words and actions?

What principles inform how you practice leadership? Write them down in your journal. Take them for a test drive. That's the only way to determine if you're walking the talk.

These first three chapters provide context for the work ahead. In the following chapters, we'll look at how you can make a bigger impact by being more intentional about how you show up, what you focus on, and what you get done. We'll establish an approach for leading people and teams into and through significant change.

To change an organization, there's only one place to start: grab a mirror.

CHAPTER 4

YOUR NEXT NORMAL

WHEN I WAS IN ELEMENTARY SCHOOL, we got a grade for our academic work as well as a "citizenship" grade. The citizenship grade had five elements: can think and act independently, follows directions, works and plays well with others, claims only their share of attention, and respects the rights and property of others. We were graded with an S for satisfactory, an N for needs improvement, or a U for unsatisfactory.

For most of grade school, I got lots of Ns for "works and plays well with others." Because my parents took the citizenship grade seriously, this became an intense topic of conversation at least four times a year. In the workplace—and everywhere, for that matter—I think we give one another citizenship grades all the time, especially in the area of "works and plays well with others." How would you be graded?

Imagine you and I are at your retirement party. I've gathered a few of your colleagues in the corner and asked them to tell me what it was like to work with you. Basically, I want to know if you worked and played well with others. I've asked them to describe your leadership style and your impact on them and the business. What are they telling me? If I asked them to come up with five words to describe you as a leader, which ones would I hear the most? Would there be a consistent theme? Would the people who reported to you answer differently than your peers or your superior?

We typically only think about these types of questions and our answers to them when prompted, perhaps in a leadership development program or by a pesky executive coach. Reflecting on such questions then discussing our answers with someone is how we continue to rethink, reset, and renew how we show up and create our next normal as leaders.

Macro-level change—change at an organizational and team level—requires micro-level change from individuals. The only individual you can change is you. The rest is leadership.

If we're going to reset our teams, create the next normal for our organizations, and help people navigate the accompanying changes, we need to start in the most logical place. We need to create our own next normal as leaders.

Rethinking, resetting, and renewing how we show up as leaders is a learning process. As adults, we learn best when we engage in an iterative, three-step process of reflection, dialogue, and practice. We're going to reflect on what you want your impact to be and your ability to activate and have that impact.

YOUR IMPACT

Think back to when you were in high school. Think of a couple of kids you knew or were friends with. You may be thinking, *Ryan was so cool, Aisha was so smart,* or *Greg was such a goofball.* You may remember certain kids as straight-arrows, troublemakers, jocks, or stoners. Even if you finished high school long ago, the stories you tell about the kids you went to school with endure. I'm not a goofball anymore, though if you haven't seen me since high school, that may be my legacy to you.

Marketers tell us the strength of a brand manifests in how precisely it manages to occupy a monopoly position in people's perception. This is achieved by condensing a brand's peak performances and conveying them in the market so that not the product but the brand triggers the purchase decision with its indispensability.

The strength of a personal brand manifests in how precisely it manages to occupy a monopoly position in people's perception by conveying our own performance (what we deliver, how we deliver, the experience we generate through our behavior) to the team and organization. We want our personal or leadership brand to trigger another person's desire to engage us, increasing the likelihood of our retention and promotion within the organization.

Usually, we talk about legacy as what we remember about people after they're gone. We talk about the legacy of our grandparents or parents, of teachers and coaches, or of historical figures we admired and looked up to. In actuality, we're leaving a legacy all the time.

Remember those folks at your retirement party? The legacy you will have left them will be based upon all the conversations you ever had and all the meetings you ever attended. You are building your brand in every interaction, every meeting, every day. Over time, the patterns become your brand. When you leave, that brand becomes your legacy. If today was your last day, how confident are you with the legacy you're leaving behind? What will you be remembered for?

People talk. As a leader, you must know that they talk about you. Probably every day. Probably right now. What are they talking about? Maybe they're discussing something you said or did in a recent meeting. Maybe they're reacting to something you decided or a change you're initiating. People walk away from every interaction with you with a story in their mind about you—what you make them think, how you make them feel. Regardless of the particulars, you can be sure people are talking among themselves about how you show up and the impact that has on them, on their team or your team, and on the business. Every day, people observe our behavior and ask themselves, *What do I think about this person as a leader?* and *Do I trust this person?*

They talk about what they observe about you and your leadership. Is she grounded or scattered? Is he open and approachable? Are they honest and sincere? Is he reliable? Does she bring great ideas and deliver great work? Are they concerned with other people's success or just their own? Does he have my back? Does she bring out the best in others? Are they a good boss or someone I'd never work for again?

They talk about your style. Is he an authoritarian, "do it my way" type? Is she transactional? Do they take a hands-off approach, or are they a micromanager? Is she democratic and inclusive? Does he take a servant leadership approach? Do they use a coach approach?

They talk about what they think you're good at and bad at, how you lead your team, and the impact you have. Is he a strong communicator? Is she a strategic thinker? Is he decisive? Does he have empathy for others? Does she focus on results and get things done?

When we become more intentional about who we are and how we approach our work and lead, we become exponentially more impactful. Maybe it's time to consider an upgrade. Continuous improvement isn't just for software; it's for people too.

If you need another reason as to why we start with you, here's one I often repeat with those I coach: when we announce a change in the organization and don't match that announcement with a simultaneous change in how we engage others and our work, people tend to not believe we are serious about change. Brené Brown, researcher and author of *Dare to Lead*, says, "When leaders expect others to change without participating and holding themselves accountable, change is almost impossible. When leaders show up and model the vulnerability for transformative change, it's often unstoppable."

Our actions impact how completely people believe and how fully they engage. Your people will emulate, replicate, and scale the style, behaviors, and practices you demonstrate. They preach your gospel.

JOURNAL TIME

It's journaling time. I want you to reflect on the following questions and prompts as a way of homing in on a clear and consistent statement about what kind of leader you want to be. Knowing that, you can identify the behaviors and practices consistent with the statement and those that are counterproductive.

1. Make a list of five people who made a positive impact as leaders. They don't have to be business leaders. Their impact could have been in sports, politics, the arts, philosophy, or religion. They could be relatives or ancestors in your family tree.

2. Think about the people on your list. What made them impactful? What words best describe them and their leadership? How did they help people? How did they adapt and respond to change?

3. Of the characteristics you've written down, which ones come up more than once? Do you have five characteristics that all of the people you chose have in common?

4. Make a note of who you'd place at the top of the list.

5. Think of that person and fill in the blanks in this statement: NAME is a _____ leader who helped others _____.

6. This person and how they showed up and helped others would appear to be an ideal for you. Let's hold on to that.

7. Let's go back to your retirement party. Ask your colleagues for five words again, but get more specific. If I asked them to come up with five descriptors of you when you're at your best and making a positive impact, what five words would I hear?

8. If I asked them to come up with five descriptors for when you're at your worst as a leader, what would they say?

9. What five words do you want to hear people use when they're describing how you lead?

10. Fill in the blanks in this statement: I am a _____ leader who helps others _____. This is your Impact Statement.

11. Try saying your Impact Statement aloud with your name at the start of it. "NAME is a _____ leader who helps others _____." How does it sound as if it's coming from someone else?

12. Ask yourself three questions:

   a. Am I content if this Impact Statement becomes my brand and legacy?

   b. What might I have to learn, unlearn, and practice to ensure this Impact Statement becomes my brand and legacy?

   c. Am I willing to disrupt the status quo (mine and others) to update my impact and make this my brand and legacy?

Remember, reflection is just the first part of rethinking something. I'd encourage you to reach out to that trusted colleague, friend, mentor, or coach and request their feedback. Is your Impact Statement true today or aspirational? How do they know? Their input will help you confirm or refine your Impact Statement.

Put your Impact Statement somewhere you will see it every day. I made my Impact Statement the subject of a daily meeting that pops up on my calendar at 7:00 a.m. and 7:00 p.m. every day. My Impact Statement is my mission as a coach to leaders and teams:

"I am a creative leader who helps others bring the best version of themselves to engaging others and leading change." I begin the day by asking, "What will I have to do to make this true today?" At the end of the day, I grade myself. Would I give myself an A, B, C, D, or F? What will I do differently tomorrow?

What will it take for you to "own it"—to really believe and behave so that you and others feel the impact of your leadership? You bring many existing strengths to how you show up and lead. You're already successful. What are you awesome at? Pick your top two. Write them down. What will you need to work on if you're going to fully "own" and succeed at living this Impact Statement? Are there things you'll have to learn or unlearn, habits you'll have to replace? Pick two. Write them down.

What is going to be the biggest barrier to you making your Impact Statement consistently true, the one thing that trips you up over and over again? How are you going to get in the way of your own success? Superman had to stay away from kryptonite; it would weaken and kill him. What's your kryptonite? Write it down.

Leaders I work with use their Impact Statement as a centering device for career, leadership, and business decisions. They use it to ensure their actions align with making the impact they desire. Even in the toughest and most stressful moments, they're able to check how they show up and lead others against the brand they want to build and the legacy they want to leave.

YOUR ABILITY TO ACTIVATE
(AND HAVE THE IMPACT YOU DESIRE)

Succeeding at the work of leadership requires competency in multiple domains. We use these skills to engage and empower others to work together to achieve shared goals. As I wrote in *Ultra Leadership*, three skills provide the foundation for all the competencies, skills, behaviors, and actions we leverage in order to lead transformation with positive impact: thinking carefully, feeling fully, and communicating effectively.

Thinking carefully requires the ability to find meaning in confusion, to be strategic, and to generate new and creative opportunities to address challenges. Careful thinking involves being able to encounter confusion, hold multiple pieces of information in memory at once, analyze each piece, and understand the relationship between the data points in order to lessen the confusion.

To feel fully means to be emotionally self-aware and capable of managing our emotions and energy in order to positively engage and interact with others. Feeling fully is all about emotional intelligence and resilience.

Communicating effectively involves designing, convening, hosting, and/or engaging in conversations vital to connecting with others, driving the business, and achieving success. To do this well, leaders must have a capacity for conversing, listening, and clearly presenting ideas to team members, stakeholders, and customers.

It is the responsibility of leadership to encourage engagement, creating the conditions that make it easy for people to enthusiastically, willingly, and repeatedly choose to give their best. Coaching can be described as a way to encourage and accelerate positive change for an individual or team. These skills—thinking carefully, feeling fully, and communicating effectively—enable you to coach others to shape their work, raise their performance, and achieve their best results.

It takes careful thinking to manage complexity and balance between long-term and short-term results. It takes careful thinking and effective communication to shape and share the enterprise vision in a way that inspires and empowers. It takes feeling fully to navigate the political landscape of the organizational structure and manage the myriad of relationships across multiple constituencies with a variety of stakeholders. These foundational skills enable you to build a strong team that collaborates with one another instead of competing against one another, creating a culture of openness, trust, cooperation, and accountability.

JOURNAL TIME

Here's another spot where you can break out the journal and reflect on how you're going about the work of leadership right now. It's a chance to rethink in order to reset.

Think about each item on this list. Rate yourself on a scale of one to five, with one meaning this item is an aspiration for you and five meaning the item is true for you all the time.

LEADING

I use personal power rather than authority to engage others.

1   2   3   4   5

I don't hesitate to cut through red tape to achieve success.

1   2   3   4   5

I will step in and lead when I encounter a void.

1   2   3   4   5

I convey a strong sense of urgency (i.e., I'm clear about what is of pressing importance).

1   2   3   4   5

I encourage others to stretch beyond what they believe they can do.

1   2   3   4   5

I am comfortable with uncertainty.

1   2   3   4   5

I seek feedback from others on my performance at least once a month.

1   2   3   4   5

I like to push the limits.

1   2   3   4   5

THINKING CAREFULLY

I can anticipate change and proactively plan to address potential objections and barriers.

1   2   3   4   5

I question assumptions as part of my decision-making process.

1   2   3   4   5

I am able to see the underlying patterns that cause problems.

1   2   3   4   5

I consider the organization's strategic intent when making decisions and prioritizing actions.

1   2   3   4   5

I carefully compare and contrast multiple options and their possible outcomes before making a decision.

1   2   3   4   5

I effectively prioritize to manage complex and competing tasks.

1   2   3   4   5

I effectively balance short-term and long-term priorities.

1   2   3   4   5

I consider other people's perspectives and points of view when making decisions.

1   2   3   4   5

I am open to learning new things.

1   2   3   4   5

I set aside time for deep thinking and learning.

1   2   3   4   5

FEELING FULLY (EMOTIONAL INTELLIGENCE)

I recognize how my emotions drive behaviors that impact my performance.

1   2   3   4   5

I have a strong capacity for managing my counterproductive impulses.

1 2 3 4 5

I can easily talk about my feelings with others.

1 2 3 4 5

I easily adapt to new challenges, adjusting my thinking and behavior in the face of change.

1 2 3 4 5

I am a self-starter, able to take action and follow through.

1 2 3 4 5

I have regular physical, emotional, and mental practices that keep me resilient.

1 2 3 4 5

My core values guide my decisions in complex situations.

1 2 3 4 5

I can sense what others are feeling and demonstrate empathy toward them.

1 2 3 4 5

I am effective at managing relationships with stakeholders across constituencies.

1   2   3   4   5

COMMUNICATING EFFECTIVELY

I consider what others need to know when designing how I communicate.

1   2   3   4   5

I am naturally curious about other people's perspectives and opinions.

1   2   3   4   5

I convey information clearly and concisely.

1   2   3   4   5

I respond to requests for my time, energy, or input in a timely manner.

1   2   3   4   5

I actively listen, giving my full attention when others are speaking.

1   2   3   4   5

I am adept at making presentations to a group.

1   2   3   4   5

I can clearly and enthusiastically enroll others to work with me to realize the (enterprise, business unit, team) vision.

1   2   3   4   5

I encourage dialogue by asking questions with a non-judgmental attitude.

1   2   3   4   5

When I help leaders with a 360-feedback process, these reflections help frame our conversations. Taken as a whole, we get a clear picture of how the leader shows up and approaches her work. Your reflection on these items is a first step. You know the drill by now. How will you confirm whether your self-assessment is accurate? What's your evidence? Go ask someone or multiple "someones." Talk it out so you can determine the one or two things you want to focus on improving in the next ninety days.

DESIGNING YOUR NEXT NORMAL

When I got up off the couch all those years ago and began mountain biking and then running, my friend told me, "When you're mountain biking, if you look at the rock, you're going to hit that rock." He was right. I tell my clients something similar, "Attention follows intention."

If you intend for your team to be more collaborative, you will place your time, energy, and resources into efforts to make that a reality. If you didn't design your team to be collaborative, you really don't expect them to be, and therefore, they aren't. Everything produces what it is designed to produce. If you want a different experience, you will need to rethink and reset what you've designed.

Practice is the only way we get better at something, and it is the only way we reset our leadership, renew the story, and upgrade our impact. When we get serious about resetting our leadership, we make a commitment to practice. The question is: practice what? Leadership takes a combination of competencies and skills. Look at your Impact Statement. To fully live your Impact Statement, what mindset will you need? What skillset will you need to tap, leverage, and hone?

What adjective did you use in your Impact Statement? "NAME is a _____ leader." What will you have to be good at and do consistently for people to use that word when describing you?

Let's focus your efforts on creating a next normal for the next ninety days. Pick something you want to reset, such as becoming more resilient. Resilience involves smart energy management.

Create a chart like this:

Things to Practice				Target
Exercise three times a week	Create space between meetings	Check-In weekly with an Account-ability Partner	Meditate five minutes each day	Be more resilient

Put your chart somewhere you'll see it every day. Enlist your assistant, a colleague, or your coach to observe you, provide feedback, and help you as you work toward your target. When seeking input about how to go about your reset from others, use what Marshall Goldsmith calls "feed forward" in his book, *What Got You Here Won't Get You There*. Find someone you trust. Tell them what you want to get better at. Ask for two suggestions you could test and practice. Say, "Thanks." Go practice.

This ninety-days-at-a-time method works to keep your development practice focused and its impact immediate. It's taken years to establish your current leadership normal; it will take time to create your next leadership normal.

Let's say you want to shift your style from authoritarian to coaching. Break that down into component parts. What mindset of coaching do you need to rethink and reset? Coaching takes too long? My job is to give direction? What skills might you need to develop? Listening? Asking great questions? Giving constructive and timely feedback? Focus your development practice every ninety days on no more than two things. Some may roll over from one quarter to the next. That's fine. That's the work.

These first four chapters have provided an opportunity for you to rethink, reset, and renew how you see the work of leadership and the impact you want to make as a leader in your organization. Leaders grow leaders. In Chapter 5, we'll go into the three broad categories of the conditions necessary for team success so you can give people what they need and get out of the way.

TRANSFORMATIVE LEADERSHIP

MANY YEARS AGO, I facilitated a conversation between the CFOs of a global organization and a group of early-career, high-potential, first-time leaders the CFOs had agreed to mentor. One of the young leaders asked for advice on what to study or learn about finance and accounting to help their careers. The answer stunned the group. Each CFO agreed the group probably knew most of what they needed to know about finance and accounting already. The CFOs were confident the group members had the functional knowledge they needed to succeed.

The CFOs said a leader's time is divided between tasks and people, and the higher you climb, the more time you spend with people. They told this group of eager twenty-somethings that as CFOs, they spent maybe 5 to 10 percent of their time looking at spreadsheets and the rest of their time in meetings influencing decisions and coaching people. They saw their responsibility was to take care of their teams. Their message was clear: if you want to accelerate your career path, lean into developing your team leadership and human skills.

To this day, I still encounter leaders who fail to grasp this lesson. They're approaching their work as if the organization is a machine and people are components or tools to be leveraged, rather than actors to be empowered. They direct by telling and see people and their "issues" as distractions.

One more time for the folks in the back: people are not a distraction; *people are your job*. The team doesn't exist to serve you; it's the other way around. Your job is to create the conditions that enable a group of people to come together, stay together, and work together willingly, enthusiastically, and repeatedly.

"Give people what they need and get out of the way"—we've all heard it from a coach or mentor at some point or shared it with a direct report who's also a people manager. So, what do people need to move forward successfully? When we travel, we may use a GPS system to help us find our way to our destination. I use the term Teamwork GPS to identify and assess the three broad categories of conditions needed for team success. They are guiding stars, provisions, and skill and will.

GUIDING STARS

People need shared clarity, or guiding stars, to align around as they work to engage and contribute to the team's important work. But first, what is a team?

In 1993, McKinsey partners Jon Katzenbach and Douglas Smith described a team as "a small number of people with complementary skills who are committed to a common purpose, set of performance goals, and approach for which they hold themselves mutually accountable." A few years later, MIT Sloan's Ralph Katz would describe a high-performing team as one that is empowered, self-directed, and cross-functional, with complementary skills and a commitment to collaboration.

You likely began your career as an individual contributor, and your success was determined by what you delivered and how well you worked with teammates and stakeholders. When you become leader of a team, your success depends on your ability to get other people to deliver things on your behalf. The higher you climb in an organization, the truer this becomes.

When I engage with a leadership team, one of the first questions I ask is, "What makes you a team?" I want to know if they share a common purpose, performance goals, and an agreement for mutual accountability. Do they collaborate to solve problems? Are they transparent with one another about what's going on in their areas or with their team? Do members of the team leverage one another as thinking partners? Do they share resources? Do they support one another's development? Most leadership teams don't function as a team. They function as a group of functional or area leaders who happen to report to the same person. They meet on a regular basis and maneuver against one another for resources. They're cordial, yet their concern is for their silo. They're a management group; they're not a team.

When I ask, "Which do you want to be? Which do you *need* to be? A group of leaders or a leadership team?" every team says, "We need to be a leadership team." With that, we've created a desire to change and agreed a gap exists. Then, the work begins.

In the process of coming together and working together, teams go through stages of development. In the 1960s, Bruce Tuckman introduced a model for understanding the stages of team development. The four stages are:

- **FORMING**: the team comes together and forms in order to deliver on shared goals.

- **STORMING**: the team negotiates the principles, practices, and processes everyone will use in order to work well together.

- **NORMING**: the team arrives at an agreement on its "ways of working"—the principles, practices, and processes everyone will use to work together to deliver on shared goals.

- **PERFORMING**: the team operates according to its agreed principles, using agreed practices and processes to get stuff done.

Most teams I've encountered put almost zero thought and intention into defining high performance *for them*. As a result, the storming process results in counterproductive practices, processes, and behaviors becoming the norm for the team, negatively impacting performance.

Our goal is for your team of leaders to become a high-performing leadership team. How do you do that? Do these four things, and you're off to a great start:

- Help the team come together and commit to working together in a productive way that generates trust, empowerment, and mutual accountability.

- Help the team align around its unique mission, shared goals, a plan for achieving those goals, and clarity of each person's role and responsibility to the team.

- Help each person shape their work by focusing their attention and time on the most important outcomes they can produce.

- Help each person achieve their best by coaching them to own their contribution and development.

Shared clarity is a sign of leadership. Teams need to agree on a vision, mission, strategy, and plan. Each member needs to know their role, responsibilities, and accountabilities. The whole team needs to be aligned on what success looks like. Shared clarity of these things makes up the guiding stars that the team and each member can use to find their way when they become disoriented or lost in the complexity and pace of the day-to-day. That high level of alignment enables smarter decision-making, easier prioritization, and quicker execution.

Assess your team's current conditions to determine the best path forward. Consider each guiding star carefully. For each statement, the only possible responses are "Yes," "Needs Work," or "No." Your

TRANSFORMATIVE LEADERSHIP

TRANSFORMATIVE LEADERSHIP

inability to answer "Yes" indicates an area where you need to take action.

- The team knows and understands our organization's vision and strategy.

- The team knows and understands our team's mission and deliverables.

- The team knows and understands their individual roles and responsibilities.

- The team knows and understands our success measures (outcomes and metrics).

- The team knows and understands who our key stakeholders are.

- The team knows and understands our individual account-abilities and contribution measurements (APOs, KPIs, and so on).

Once you and your team have agreed on your guiding stars, it's time to provide everyone with the provisions they need for success.

PROVISIONS

In the age of industry, when we thought of organizations as machines, we just needed hands to work the assembly line. Now that we're in an age of information and we see organizations as living systems, the game has changed. We need to tap into what's in people's heads. We need people who think carefully and bring creativity to their work.

People need the right provisions to achieve their objectives: a positive environment and culture, efficient structure, simple processes and tools, and adequate resources. A well-resourced team with rituals and routines that enable performance and productivity is a sign of leadership.

Leaders have to say, "Here's what we're hoping to accomplish. I trust you have the knowledge and skill to figure out what to do." Trust is the most important provision—you won't get far without a culture of mutual trust. You must ask: Do we trust we are open to working with one another? Do we trust we are being sincere with one another? Do we trust one another's reliability? Do we believe one another to be competent and good at what they do? Do we trust that we have one another's backs as we go about our work?

Another important provision for the journey is a commitment to and process for open and honest communication between and among team members. David Isaacs and Juanita Brown, co-originators of *The World Café*, see conversation as a core business process. We come together, stay together, and work together through the quality of the conversations we have with one another. A culture of openness and honest communication facilitates creating and sustaining strong alignment and high engagement.

Positive leadership is another important provision. People watch everything you do, which makes what you *do* much more important than what you *say*. It's up to you as leader of the team to walk the walk and model the behaviors you expect your team to demonstrate.

Other provisions critical to the team's journey are the systems, processes, and tools the team has access to in order to deliver their accountabilities. For example, one vital process is a clearly-defined work breakdown structure such as RACI (RACI = Responsible/ Accountable/Consulted/Informed).

Consider each item. Is your answer, "Yes," "Needs Work," or "No"?

- We have a foundation of trust within our team that enables effective cooperation to get things done.

- We have a culture of openness and honest communication that facilitates strong alignment and high engagement.

- We are supported with efficient and effective systems and processes.
- We have access to a variety of productivity, leadership, and teamwork tools.
- We have a clearly-defined work breakdown structure (RACI).
- We have leaders, including me, who provide strong positive examples to follow.

Because no one aims for mediocre, let's now build the individual and collective capacity of your team to establish a state of constant readiness and high performance.

SKILL AND WILL

I haven't worked with a team yet that hasn't wanted to go fast and win. As the leader of the team, your role is to create the conditions for this group of people to go as fast as possible toward their shared goals and winning as they've defined it.

Imagine your team is setting sail on a journey. There is a skipper, a leader of the whole boat—that's you. As the journey is underway, the act of leading moves around the boat. Each crew member is empowered and trusted to lead from their position in the moment it is needed. Each crew member is accountable for acting in the right way, in the right moment, in order for the team to achieve its shared goal: to reach the destination.

In this environment, the leader needs the team and each member to bring their best. It's up to the leader to align everyone on what's most important, to ensure that the team and each individual has the capacity and resources to engage, contribute, and coordinate all the activity into a productive process.

People need the competence to perform and work with others as part of a team. They need something meaningful to connect them to the work and their colleagues. They need the aptitude and attitude, the skill and will, to succeed.

Once again, consider whether the following statements are true for your team or need work:

- The team has the functional skills and abilities to engage, contribute, and deliver on their accountabilities to achieve our mission.

- The team has the leadership and teamwork skills and abilities that enable us to work together in pursuit of our shared goals.

- The team has the emotional and social intelligence to build and sustain strong relationships.

- The team has the means to manage conflicts in productive and positive ways.

- We have a mechanism for regular and ongoing feedback between and among team members.

- The team demonstrates a willingness to adjust plans and approaches to implementing our strategy.

Your answers for each of these sets of statements may not match up 100 percent with your team's answers. When it comes to skill and will, balance is important. All the skills in the world are useless without the will to use those skills on behalf of the team's shared goals. And, as much as you may want to do something, without the necessary skills, it's probably not going to happen.

Wherever your team is starting from, it's your responsibility as a leader to create and sustain the conditions for success. Your leadership ensures the team has guiding stars to align on, provisions to sustain them, and the skill and will to keep moving and reach their destination. Now, let's create your team's next normal.

CHAPTER 6

YOUR TEAM'S NEXT NORMAL

AS I WRITE THIS, I AM just traveling home from a quarterly meeting with a leadership team I coach at a Fortune 500 company. I love this team. Everyone exhibits a growth mindset and fully embraces the work of shaping the next normal for themselves, for the team as a whole, and for their people, teams, and organization.

When we began our work, they decided that, to shape the next normal for the organization, they needed to dedicate themselves to the work of rethinking and resetting in a way that is noticeable to their people and teams. They knew it would be a journey. They also know they've passed the point of no return. Their work is to build an organization that excels at transformation, and, as their next normal continues to take shape, they're succeeding.

Let's create your team's next normal. What do you want to see when you look around? The most successful teams always know where they are going. They are always getting better. They interact in a highly coordinated way. You want to see a team aligned around some clear guiding stars, well-provided for, with the skill and will to cooperate and collaborate to deliver on shared goals.

Either you're making it easy for people to work together, or you're not. When I work with leaders and their teams, we align on their shared business priorities. We establish commitments for building the team's capacity to cooperate and collaborate in order to execute and deliver their priorities. We coordinate action by empowering each person to set their near-term deliverables and development goals. We set a cadence for regular team meetings to review progress against priorities and commitments, and we conduct 1:1s using their deliverables and development goals as context.

Your job is to ensure the conditions in which the team works are created by design and not by default. The same three practices that make an organization change-worthy help you fulfill your responsibility as leader of a team. Again, it's not rocket science; it's as simple as ABC: Align People, Build Bench Strength, and Coordinate Action.

ALIGN PEOPLE

When I was a kid, there were always a bunch of maps in the glove compartment of the car. If we got lost, my mom or dad took out a map and looked at it to see where we were and to figure out the best, fastest, and safest route to our destination.

I use Team Roadmaps for a similar purpose: to help teams align around their guiding stars. These guiding stars include vision, mission, strategy, execution plan, roles, accountabilities, and success measures. I employ Team Roadmaps as an important part of a leadership and team management system that aligns people, builds bench strength, and coordinates action.

When completed, the Team Roadmap is a "plan on a page," indicating your mission, your key results or success measures (priorities), your objectives, and your workstream stewards. If anyone should forget the team's mission or where the team is going, all they would need to do is to look at the Team Roadmap to jog their memory. Here's what the Team Roadmap looks like:

TEAM ROADMAP

Mission:			Key Results (Success Measures)	
Stewards	Objectives / Big Rocks (6 max)		Outcomes	Metrics
			Business	
			Team	

TEAM ROADMAP TEMPLATE

As a leader, it's a good idea for you to think through the Team Roadmap sections on your own first. You should be able to clearly state the team's unique mission and the outcomes your team needs to deliver. However, I caution you to resist the temptation to complete the Roadmap yourself and share it with your team. We don't want the team to buy into your Roadmap—we want the team to co-own their Roadmap.

When I'm working with a team for the first time, it can take them a couple of days to generate a first cut of their Team Roadmap. Teams that use the tool and process regularly get faster with each iteration.

Here's how you could align people using a Team Roadmap:

ALIGN

Invite your team to a meeting with the purpose of aligning around a clear mission that makes your strategic priorities evident.

FOCUS YOUR MISSION

Every team has a distinct mission, empowered to deliver certain outcomes no other team in your organization owns. What is your team's unique mission? Why does your team exist? What is your team responsible for delivering? What work won't get done if your team doesn't do it? How does your team's mission support the broader mission of your business unit or organization?

You'll notice there's not much space in this section of the Roadmap template. That's intentional. Being concise and keeping your team mission to a single sentence or phrase will go a long way—not only helping your team remember what you are all here to do but also when talking to and collaborating with other teams.

SET A TIMEFRAME

You're not going to achieve your mission overnight. Most teams I work with set a period of six months to a year as a workable timeframe. This helps keep the work strategic in nature. The longer timeframe elevates their thinking and helps them engage in more robust prioritization.

DEFINE SUCCESS

What key results do you want to achieve? Setting success measures is probably the hardest but most important part of creating your Team Roadmap. This section has two parts: outcomes and metrics. When you begin to think about outcomes, you'll try and stuff five pounds of work in a three-pound bag. Don't do it. Within your chosen timeframe, what are the top business outcomes your team must produce to declare success? There's a subtle but important distinction here. Your outcomes should not be tasks. Tasks or activities produce an outcome. Your outcomes are the result of the work your team does day in and day out. If you're struggling with identifying outcomes, think of your team's mission. For your team to declare "mission accomplished," what outcomes must you achieve? There is intentionally only space for five business outcomes in the Team Roadmap. You might be tempted to add more, but you should challenge yourself to keep it to five. Relentlessly prioritizing your work on the highest impact outcomes is critical to mission success and team health.

Let's talk metrics. How will you know you've achieved each outcome? How will you measure success? For each outcome, what are the one or two most important metrics that you will use to define success? Metrics can be quantitative. Maybe one of your metrics is a revenue or expense target, such as, "We achieved a 10 percent increase in customer growth;" maybe it's an increase in a customer or employee satisfaction score. Metrics can also be qualitative, such as securing buy-in from senior management on a strategic plan. The power of articulating outcomes and metrics is the team's strong alignment on its shared goals. It's clear to everyone on the team, "Here's what we are going to deliver, and here's how we will know when we've done it."

The sixth row on your Team Roadmap is reserved for an outcome specific to the state of the team. Let's say you achieved your business outcomes, but your team is a mess. People have quit. People are exhausted. Relationships within the team are stressed or damaged. That's not the kind of next normal you want to create or work in. To declare success, you need the team and its members to be engaged, energized, and ready for the next six months or year. That's why there's room on your Team Roadmap for a team outcome. What's the team outcome you want to achieve, and how will you measure that outcome?

OBJECTIVES OR "BIG ROCKS"

Once you've agreed on the success measures as a team, the next step is to determine what must happen to achieve each outcome. What work has to occur? There are multiple projects, tasks, initiatives, or actions that come together to produce your stated outcome. This is where you prioritize. What will you do? What won't you do?

- Notice there are only six spaces in each row. Take all the projects, tasks, initiatives, and actions; group them into no more than six buckets. We call those the "big rocks." Some big rocks may be one major project or initiative. Other big rocks may be a grouping of projects, tasks, initiatives, or actions.

- The big rocks form a workstream leading to each outcome. The team should be able to look at the big rocks in a workstream and agree that, "If we do these things, we will deliver this outcome and hit these metrics." Eventually, each team member should be able to look at the Team Roadmap and see how their role and what they deliver contribute to the team's shared goals.

STEWARDS

When you've agreed on what success looks like, and you've identified the big rocks you'll need to move to achieve each outcome, the next step is to identify someone on the team to "steward" each workstream.

Stewardship doesn't mean that team member is responsible for all the work associated with an outcome and its big rocks. To steward a workstream is to agree to convene other team members (as well as representatives of other teams) as needed, to scope the work, and to be the primary person to report on progress at regular review meetings. Identify a primary and backup steward for each workstream.

The process of collaborating to build and use a Team Roadmap produces alignment and accountability. It might take you a few meetings to agree on a final product. That's okay—it is better to spend the time up front getting aligned as a team than it is to find out after the fact that you worked on things that were not contributing to the broader business unit or organizational vision and goals.

Once you and your team feel good about the Team Roadmap you've put together, you should share it. Share it with your manager to confirm the two of you are in alignment on what your team is working on and set to deliver. Share it with your peers, stakeholders, and support partners outside of your function, business unit, or division. Transparency and inclusion invite collaboration and support.

TEAM ROADMAP-HR LEADERSHIP TEAM 2022

Mission: Lead Organizational Evolution to Accelerate Customer Centricity						Key Results (Success Measures)	
Stewards	Objectives / Big Rocks (6 max)					Outcomes	Metrics
Steve, Kate	Goal Setting: Performance & Development	System Workday Navigate	360e Feedback	Quarterly Check-ins	Rating & Rewards	**Business** Performance Management	100% Adoption by All People Managers
Rajiv, Carol	Values Next Steps	Key Behaviors & Practices	LA Next Steps	Comms Strategy	Engage Leadership	Winning Culture	E-Sat Is Up / Retention Is Up
Beth, Joe	Socialize Mgr. Dev. Profile	Create Development Path	Establish Manager Community	Tools and Resources	Manager Development Program	Manager Development	Rollout commenced Q3
Karen, Chris	Consulting Process	Online Learning	Onboarding	LD Offsite	Development Days	Performance Culture	Survey Partners
Francesca, Anthony	Identify Key Roles	Scoping	Talent Review Process	Succession Plans	BoD	Talent	Leadership Sign-off on Talent Strategy / Rollout Underway
Theresa, Larry	Roles/RACI	Model of Accountability	Individual Development	Expand Virtual Team	Quarterly Team Offsites	**Team** Improved Bench Strength	Achieved Business Outcomes / Pulse Survey Up

SAMPLE COMPLETED TEAM ROADMAP

Use your Team Roadmap as a focal point to keep your team aligned. Establish a good cadence to review your team's progress on executing your Team Roadmap. Most teams convene a monthly review meeting. I use a RAG (red, amber, green) system to report on status.

- Green: all work is on-track.

- Amber: we're stuck, but we have options. We need to test options and decide the best course of action to proceed.

- Red: we're stuck, and we lack a solution. We need to discuss or schedule a separate meeting to address the situation and come up with a plan.

Your review meetings should be no more than two hours. When your Team Roadmap is first completed, consider every outcome and big rock "red." Stewards prepare for each meeting by engaging key partners or stakeholders and doing a RAG assessment of each big rock and outcome. Each steward will come to the first review meeting having reset the status to amber or green if possible.

Whatever you decide, it's important that you commit to a cadence and stay consistent in your approach. It's at these regular review meetings the team will share and agree to necessary adjustments as plans or priorities change.

A tool is a device to help us accomplish a task; it is a means to an end. Processes are ways we complete tasks. The Team Roadmap is both a tool and a process you can use to create shared clarity and sustain alignment. Once your team is aligned, what behaviors and practices will they need to demonstrate in order to follow the Team Roadmap and fulfill their mission?

BUILD BENCH STRENGTH

One of your responsibilities as a leader is to build bench strength—the organizational, team, and individual capacity to execute and deliver on the organization's and team's shared goals. You must make sure the team and each individual have what they need in order to achieve their best.

It doesn't matter if you're new to the team or if you've brought on a new member—every change to the makeup of the team is an experience of re-forming. Change one person, and it's a new team. The dynamic shifts. The web of relationships changes.

New teams need to align on ways of working that encourage cooperation and collaboration. Remember, your goal is a high-performing leadership team, not a team of leaders working as a management group. This means helping the team come together and commit to working in a productive way that generates trust, empowerment, and mutual accountability.

Call a meeting with your team. Tell them the purpose of the meeting is to commit to high performance, as defined by the team. Ask them to do some reflection as pre-work. Have each team member consider:

- What is a team?
- What do high-performing teams have in common?
- What does high performance look like?
- If we want to be a high-performing team, what behaviors do we need to commit to?
- What are your top five suggestions for behaviors that, if everyone exhibited them, the team would meet the definition of high-performance?
- Which behavior is a strength for you?
- Which behavior poses a development opportunity for you?

The meeting should take anywhere from ninety minutes to two hours. At the meeting, welcome the team. Set the stage by reminding them about the purpose of the meeting: to be more intentional about the normal the team creates and operates in.

Your role during the meeting is to ask questions. These are their team commitments. They are the team; you are the team leader. Your inquiry is to confirm that they believe the commitments they align on as a way of working together will enable them to stay engaged with one another and get stuff done.

With everyone welcomed, open a discussion about the pre-work. Ask team members about their experience doing the pre-work. Ask each person to share their list of five suggested behaviors. Ask each to identify which of their five they think is most important. You'll end up with a good list of behaviors. There will be some duplication. That's a good thing; it shows where there is alignment about what it will take to be a high-performing team.

Next, ask the team to sort through the aggregated list and begin to winnow it down. Task them to generate a list of five behaviors representing the core of their next normal. Give each person the opportunity to make the case for a behavior they think is important. Eventually, you'll ask them to vote and arrive at a final list of five commitments that complete the statement, "We will _____."

I've done this exercise with many teams. Here is a sampling of team commitments:

- Practice Radical Prioritization
- Speak Our truth (Note: the "t" in truth is intentionally lowercase to remind us that our truth is not The Truth; it's *our* truth.)
- Run as One
- Practice Accountability
- Discuss, Decide, and Go
- Drive Change
- Be a "No Victim" Zone
- Be Mission Focused and Outcome Driven
- Think "We," Not "Me"
- Have a Preference for Action
- Communicate Honestly, Openly, Directly
- Challenge Each Other Respectfully
- Keep Our Customers at the Table
- Stay Focused (Avoid Shiny Objects)
- Advocate for One Another

- Be Consciously Curious
- Seek to Understand
- GGSD (Get Great "Stuff" Done)
- Lean into Hard Conversations
- Give and Receive Feedback Openly
- Have One Another's Back
- Stay Aligned
- Solve Problems Together
- Assume Positive Intent
- Enjoy the Ride
- Be Open and Honest with One Another
- Be Aligned on Strategy and Outcomes
- Be Transparent
- Be Collaborative
- Break Down Silos

When your team has agreed upon their set of commitments, remind them that we measure what's important. At this point, you can help them determine their baseline. Are the commitments they are making true today or completely aspirational? Have the team rate themselves against each commitment. On a scale of one to five, with one being low and five being high, how well are they living up to each commitment? Add their scores and find the average. That's your starting point.

With a baseline score in hand, you can help the team brainstorm to come up with some ideas for bumping their score for each commitment. Ask, "What's one thing we could do to raise our performance against each commitment?" Pick one concrete, repeatable action that you, as team leader, can put in place to help the team be accountable to their commitments. Moving forward, make sure the team revisits their commitments on a regular basis. Some teams I work with revisit their commitments whenever they review their Team Roadmap. Some teams choose a quarterly cadence. Whatever you and your team choose, make it your responsibility to keep the commitments real and relevant to how everyone shows up and works with one another. Make the commitments the "norm" for how the team performs.

Establishing team commitments and convening regular conversations about progress against each commitment is a simple and repeatable way to build individual and collective capacity. Intentional, regular focus on the behaviors and practices associated with the team's definition for high-performance influences each individual's development goals. This enables you to provide each team member with coaching as they consider how best to close their knowledge and skill gaps and accelerate their development.

What education, experience, or exposure does each person need or want to pursue in order to grow their capacity to engage and contribute? Helping each person get better builds bench strength. Engaging each individual and the team in these capacity and development conversations is a demonstration of three of your principles in action: leading is a balancing act; you're a coach, not a machine operator; and to win is to learn and serve.

With the team aligned around its guiding stars and committed to working together to meet its own definition of high performance, how do you coordinate all the activity and ensure nothing falls through the cracks? How do you ensure your people are working on the right things each quarter, are productive and not just busy, and are continuing their individual development? This is the third practice you're responsible for: helping your team work together in a coordinated way.

COORDINATE ACTION

Empowered people and teams are productive. You've taken a step toward building an empowered team by aligning your team members around a Team Roadmap, enabling people to say:

- "I understand the team's mission."
- "I understand what's most important."
- "I understand what needs to be done."
- "I understand my role and responsibility."

You're adding to the team's empowerment by engaging them to set commitments for high performance. Now, how do you coordinate the activity that alignment produces and encourage greater autonomy and self-direction with each team member?

The teams I work with use a tool called a Tactical Action Plan (TAP) to coordinate action while encouraging ongoing personal and professional development. TAPs are an important ingredient in our recipe. Individual TAPs are a personal empowerment tool for creating alignment, focus, and accountability while helping the team leader keep the team's efforts coordinated.

- TAPs ensure alignment. To create and work from a TAP, team members begin looking more regularly at your team's shared goals and objectives as reflected in the Team Roadmap. When team members are aligned with the team's shared goals, it becomes easier for each person to prioritize and shape their work.

- TAPs also ensure greater focus. Your team members have a lot on their plates. How do they decide where to place their time and attention in order to make the biggest impact? How do they decide what to focus on and what to say "yes" or "no" to when considering requests for their time and energy?

- TAPs ensure accountability. What work is each team member responsible for and accountable to deliver? While the Team Roadmap is more of a strategic document, articulating outcomes and objectives for six months or a year, TAPs confirm the outcomes each person is accountable to deliver in the short term, quarter by quarter.

- TAPs empower your team. A TAP allows each team member to more confidently have trade-off conversations with you or their peers and make aligned decisions about where to place their time, energy, and resources. That is empowering. Working from a TAP, they have the power to say "no" or "not now" to *good* work so they can say "yes" to *great* work.

- TAPs create psychological safety. A TAP establishes an agreement between you and each team member as to what work they will contribute each quarter. It enables them to respond to surprises or "fire drills" with greater alignment and a capacity to prioritize new requests in consultation with you.

TAPs also remind each person to keep working on getting better. Where the Team Roadmap has an outcome focusing on the state of the team, the TAP includes space for two personal development goals. It is critical each member of the team focus on their own continuous development as a person and as a leader in their own right. Keeping development goals front and center helps drive accountability and better enables managers and peers to support growth.

TACTICAL ACTION PLAN

Name:				Quarter:
ACTIONS (What must happen to achieve each Outcome?)				**MY OUTCOMES** (What will you focus on delivering?)
				MY DEVELOPMENT GOALS

TACTICAL ACTION PLAN (TAP) TEMPLATE

With your Team Roadmap as a guide, coach each individual on your team to create their own TAP. When you're coaching someone to generate their TAP, keep in mind that the plan is theirs, not yours. You're helping them *identify* their outcomes, not *giving them* their outcomes.

Outcomes are what they will own and complete in the next ninety days. These are things that can be realistically accomplished and will be their priorities in the near term. If there is an outcome they will delegate to someone else, they should not include it; that outcome belongs in that person's TAP. The TAP is an individual planning tool. What work belongs to them? What will they be accountable to deliver? That's what goes in their TAP.

Help them to identify up to four outcomes that are tangible signs of success. The more specific their outcomes, the more useful the TAP will be to them. Initially, their outcomes may only show incremental progress over a short period of time, but as they string together a series of rolling TAPs, their progress will become evident.

Next, help them fill in the Actions section. To achieve each outcome, what must happen? What tasks will they have to undertake? What conversations or meetings will they have to convene? Help them think of all the things they'll have to do to achieve each outcome. But remember, keep it simple. There should be no more than four tasks or actions for each outcome. This will enable them to stay laser-focused on their outcomes and prioritize where they place their attention and how they spend their time.

With their outcomes and actions set, help them focus on their development goals. Their development goals will depend on what their outcomes are and where you would like to improve. You might ask, "To deliver your outcomes, succeed in your role, and accelerate your path to your next role, what do you want or need to get better at? What are the two most important developmental areas you want to focus on?" You might have some ideas about performance gaps and development opportunities for each team member. This is where you can offer your observations and suggestions.

Help your team members determine what they will do to work on each development goal. Think in terms of education, experience, and exposure. For example, is it reading or listening to a podcast? Working with a coach? Shadowing another leader or executive? Setting an exercise routine or meditation practice? Development goals could also be personal, like becoming more resilient or physically fit. They might pick a leadership goal, like getting better at delegating and coaching. Again, they should enter no more than four actions that represent the new practices, routines, or rituals they'll engage in to achieve each development goal.

When you and your team members are aligned on their TAP outcomes and actions, the TAP becomes a promise of accountability for them and a way for you to simultaneously support them and ensure all your team's actions are coordinated with one another. Use the TAP as a focal point for your regular 1:1s, ensuring you and your team members are talking about the right topics. They're accountable to deliver the listed outcomes; you're accountable to coach and support.

TACTICAL ACTION PLAN

Name: James T. Kirk				**Quarter:** Q1 FY23
ACTIONS (What must happen to achieve each Outcome?)				**MY OUTCOMES** (What will you focus on delivering?)
Recruit (Advertise Position)	Interviews (by 31 May)	Decide, Offer, Hire (by 15 Jun)	Onboard & Map 1st 90 Days (01 Jul)	New Manager Onboard
Align Team on FY22 Roadmap (by 30 Apr)	Coach All Team Members to Create TAPs (by 15 May)	Set New Team Governance Cadence (Huddles & 1:1s)	Lead Monthly Roadmap Reviews	Team Aligned
Align on Target Operating Model	Select Initial Use Case	Move Analytics Resources Close to the Business	Develop Plan to Organize Data Products and Services	New Analytics Target Operating Model Agreed & Operational
Process Design (by 30 Apr)	Comms Plan (by 30 Apr)	New Process Training (by 31 May)	Adoption Support & Tracking (30 Jun - Q2)	Migration to New UX Process Complete
Read Book on Coaching	Reset All 1:1s to Use the TAP Coaching Framework	Practice Coaching with Training Partner	Get Feedback on Listening & Inquiry Skills	**MY DEVELOPMENT GOALS** Be a Good Coach
Exercise 3x a Week	Create Space between Meetings	Check-in With Partner	5 Minutes of Meditation Each Day	Be More Resilient

SAMPLE COMPLETED TAP

You should also have a TAP of your own. What work is yours this quarter? What will you deliver? Where will you place your time, energy, and attention? You get a lot of meeting requests. TAPs are valuable in reducing calendar clutter. It becomes easier to decide which invites to accept and which to decline or delegate when you have clarity of what is most important each quarter. Also, asking your team to use TAPs and not using one yourself is a bit, "Do as I say, not as I do." If you want your team to use TAPs, model the practice.

After taking the three steps laid out in this chapter, we will see the conditions for a group of leaders to come together and create a next normal, where they stay together and work together as a leadership team.

This type of team needs a different type of leader. In earlier chapters, we've talked about your impact and your next normal. In the next chapter, we'll put a finer point on what kind of leader your team needs. If you're following the recipe of this chapter, you're putting a system in place that's building an empowered team with people shaping their work and delivering on your behalf. This kind of team doesn't need a manager. This team needs a coach.

CHAPTER 7

BE A GOOD COACH

A TERRIFIC LEADER I HAVE WORKED WITH HAD, for years, been giving his team of senior leaders their annual objectives. He's not alone; there are many leaders who think that's their job. Once he aligned his team around a clear Team Roadmap, he had a choice to make. He could continue his practice of spending his Christmas holiday drawing up objectives for all his direct reports, or he could ask his team to look carefully at the Team Roadmap for the new year and generate a first draft of their objectives. He chose to rethink and reset his annual practice, creating a next normal with his team.

He discovered that what they came up with was almost identical to what he was thinking. There was only divergence when they thought of something he hadn't. The objectives they came up with eventually took the form of individual TAPs and Team Roadmaps with the teams they led. He worked with them to amend as necessary. In a coaching session not long after his experience, he proclaimed, "I'll never spend my Christmas holiday working on objectives again. Now I can show up as a coach to my team. It's an awesome and scary feeling."

In 2008, Google launched *Project Oxygen* to identify what its most successful managers do to engage people and lead high-performing teams. In 2018, they revisited their work, updated their research, and amended their list to update two behaviors and add two more. Here's the amended list:

1. Be a good coach.

2. Empower; don't micromanage.

3. Create an inclusive team environment, showing concern for success and well-being.

4. Be productive and results-oriented.

5. Be a good communicator—listen and share information.

6. Support career development and discuss performance.

7. Have a clear vision/strategy for the team.

8. Have key technical skills to help advise the team.

9. Collaborate across the organization.

10. Be a strong decision-maker.

(3 and 6 were updated; 9 and 10 were added in 2018).

These ten behaviors, or some variation of them, align with the leadership practices we've mentioned repeatedly in these pages: align people, build bench strength, and coordinate action. The *Project Oxygen* team also identified the most important activity for successful leadership and team management, which leads to stronger engagement and higher performance: be a good coach.

Empowered people don't need to or want to be told what to do, but they are open to coaching. Through coaching, we drive business results and the development of others.

LEADER-COACH MINDSET

Think of the coach of a successful sports team. Certain names come to mind: John Wooden, Steve Kerr, Tara VanDerveer, Alex Ferguson, Billie Moore. These great coaches are not on the court or pitching with the players; they are on the sidelines, teaching and guiding the thoughts and actions of the players. They try on a regular basis to push players to go beyond their limits and to willingly, enthusiastically, and repeatedly give their best, especially over the course of a long season or in challenging game conditions. When players voluntarily show up and give their best despite external challenges, their desire to engage and ability to deliver are a reflection and result of real leadership.

In this context, the definitions of leader and coach are interchangeable. Coaching can be described as a way to encourage and accelerate positive change for an individual or team. An even simpler definition of coaching is *to enable positive transformation*. Isn't this the work of leadership? This simple definition is apt because our organizations, teams, and individuals are all constantly seeking ongoing positive transformation.

In the next normal, our organizations will accelerate to become more matrixed and flatter, with teams becoming more self-directed and empowered. Leaders of teams need to pivot from being experts in their function to being experts at leadership in general and at coaching individuals and teams in particular.

To lead and coach people, we must meet them where they are. To do that, we must be conscious, connected, and concerned.

Considering the pace and pressure we face in business, it is easy for us to slip into unconsciousness. We can easily find ourselves living and working on autopilot, taking a tick-the-box approach, racing from quarter to quarter with a narrow and shortsighted view of what to do, creating flat and tepid results. It's hard to coach someone if we're unconscious.

In an age of technological hyper-connectedness, it is funny how easy it is to become disconnected from one another. The experience for too many of us during the COVID-19 pandemic was to shrink the circle of concern we create for other people. To protect ourselves from discomfort, many of us began to let less and less in. Some adopted an "I've got mine; you get yours" attitude. Many have put their heads in the sand.

If we do this as leaders, our people can view this as an indication that we value them extrinsically for what they produce and not intrinsically for who they are. They develop a sense, justified in many cases, that they are disposable. It's hard to coach someone without feeling true concern for them; it's highly improbable we would take the time and make the effort to coach them in the first place.

Greater consciousness and awareness of interconnection lead us to be genuinely concerned for others. As leaders and coaches, we must leverage this concern, using our communication skills and emotional intelligence.

Communicating effectively involves designing, convening, hosting, and/or engaging in conversations vital to connecting with others, driving the business, and achieving success. To do this well, leaders must have a capacity for conversing, listening, and clearly presenting ideas to team members, stakeholders, and customers. Everything that happens in business happens as a result of a conversation. Through conversation, leaders facilitate the individual and collective thinking that enables positive transformation. Through conversation, when we look to coach, we are doing the very same thing.

When we look to coach, listening is fundamental. Actor and writer Alan Alda says, "Real listening is a willingness to let the person change you." Real listening requires real presence and real focus. We must be conscious (in the moment), connected (focused on the person), and concerned (invested in their development and success). Only then is our listening active and authentic. Active and full listening is nonjudgmental, unconditionally constructive, and totally for the person we are coaching. Active and full listening provides the clues the leader, as coach, needs to ask the right question, in the right way, in the right moment. Without active and full listening, there can be no true coaching.

Strong listening skills are also vital to another aspect of coaching: asking powerful questions. Coaching is, first and foremost, a process of inquiry. We need to be able to frame questions that encourage reflection and dialogue. The questioning process is one of the main methods we can use to help a person find their own answers. When we look to coach, we use the questioning process to help someone; the person does the work and therefore discovers and/or provides their own answers, instead of us providing the answers for them. The true value of coaching is in the person "owning" their solutions within the coaching process.

FIVE COACHING TENETS

Pivoting to a coach approach to leadership and team management means shifting our mindset. There are five tenets vital to successfully adopting the mindset of a leader-coach:

- Look to Learn
- Look to Make Positive Assumptions
- Look to Use Inquiry before Advocacy
- Look to Enable Transformation versus Seeking Information
- Look to Coach the Person, Not the Problem

LOOK TO LEARN

Leaders achieve their position in large part because they are recognized for what they know and what they are able to do. Organizations reward high-performing individual contributors by promoting them to management roles. When you are rewarded for "knowing," you can forget to keep "learning."

If we're going to look to coach others, we need to look to learn. We need to be intentionally and intensely curious. We cannot coach someone if we believe we already "know" them, their situation, and their solution. If that's our starting position, we are going to use coaching as a premise to tell them what they need to do. When we look to coach, we look to learn from the person we are coaching.

LOOK TO MAKE POSITIVE ASSUMPTIONS

When a person isn't performing, typically, our first inclination is to believe something's wrong with them. When we look to coach, we actually go there last. The starting point for coaching is the assumption of positive intent and ability. We have to believe the person we are coaching has both the drive and the aptitude to achieve success on their own. We are coaching them to enable their success to come more quickly and more completely.

LOOK TO USE INQUIRY BEFORE ADVOCACY

When we advocate, we are telling someone what we would do or what he or she should do. Leading with advocacy results in two horrible situations. First, we become the "solution-provider," and without us, activity can grind to a halt. This is a hard habit to break because we love solving people's problems for them; we love being indispensable. Second, and even worse, we may be unwittingly communicating that we don't believe the person could come up with the solution themselves (a negative assumption), often creating or strengthening a belief within the person that they lack talent. Either way, we are left with a disempowered and disengaged person. Using inquiry before advocacy means asking more questions to invite curiosity and facilitate development, which will ultimately drive business results.

LOOK TO ENABLE TRANSFORMATION VERSUS SEEKING INFORMATION

When we ask questions seeking only information, the implicit message is that the person, team, organization, or system is a problem to be fixed and solved and that, if we have enough information, we can solve the problem for them. It's our impatience and addiction to being the expert problem-solver that drives us to hunt for clues, but we are not detectives on a case. That focus of inquiry is disempowering and threatens the status of the person (or team) as a positive contributor. We want to ask questions that enable transformation of the situation, the person, or the team.

LOOK TO COACH THE PERSON, NOT THE PROBLEM

When we look to coach, our goal is to develop the person, not only solve the problem. We are engaging with them in order to enable their positive transformation. Through our coaching, they may become more aligned with the vision and mission of the team, clearer about their unique role, and better able to think through challenges and solve problems in order to engage and contribute in a positive way.

Developing a mindset shaped by these five tenets will lead us to engage differently. When we look to coach rather than dictate, we tap into different and underutilized skills and practices.

COACHING TRAINING WHEELS

Using a coach approach is new to many leaders. We have to change the habits we formed around our love of being expert problem-solvers and choosing expeditiousness and efficiency over effectiveness and development. As we establish a next normal with our teams and begin to practice a new way of leadership and team management, we may need some training wheels to keep us from falling over and giving up. Tools can serve as training wheels as we work to develop our coaching skills. We can benefit from having an easy-to-follow process for convening coaching conversations for development and performance. Let's look at what we need to keep in mind as we design, convene, and host our coaching conversations.

COACHING CONVERSATIONS

We need to design our coaching conversations around identifying and overcoming behavioral or situational issues to encourage personal growth, rather than fixing the problem alone or chastising a person for acting a certain way. We begin by exploring what contribution they are working toward and what experience they want to have at work. This information will open the door for you to provide feedback and coaching on how to more closely align their perception with reality (from your perspective) and encourage their commitment to change.

Inquiry through masterful questioning works in tandem with active listening to shape the bulk of any coaching conversation. Masterful questions come from hearing the other person well. They are open questions that invite exploration, evoke discovery, and stimulate deeper examination and reflection. Most questions that can be answered "yes" or "no" are not masterful; we ask those questions when we are looking for information so we can solve the problem. We ask open questions when we aren't trying to solve the problem; we are interested in facilitating the other person's transformation so they can solve the problem themselves.

Good meetings begin with a clear understanding of what we want to achieve: to enable the positive transformation of the person we are coaching. We need to know the facts about the situation and the person we are coaching so we can make decisions about how to structure the conversation, what style we choose, and what coaching or leadership tools we utilize.

When we convene a coaching conversation, we are responsible for creating and maintaining the environment that will enable success. We decide the most appropriate time and place to have the conversation and whether the meeting needs to be in a formal or informal setting. Some moments and situations lend themselves to using a coach approach, such as conversations around performance, productivity, contribution management, and personal development. But some situations call for highly directive leadership, or worse, some form of disciplinary action—these situations are not conducive to a coach approach.

As host of the conversation, we are responsible for the process more than the content. The person we are coaching owns the agenda and outcome. We are trying to enable their positive transformation through this conversation, not ours. We must trust the person's intention and competence, assuming the person is willing and able to succeed. An important piece of the coach approach is the capacity to get the other person to create their own positive change. What will they do? When will they do it? Their commitment to take action is a sign that they understand how they alone own their results and their experience.

Let's look at two ways to convene coaching conversations in a way that flows from the leader-coach mindset and follows the five coaching tenets.

A³ COACHING MODEL

I developed a simple mental model for careful thinking and coaching that's more fully explained in *Ultra Leadership*. This model, called A³, is a leadership tool that helps us frame our coaching conversations by laying out three steps for careful thought, effective communication, and coaching: Aim, Align, and Act.

Step one is to "Aim." Aiming is seeing the person and their reality and sensing how that is impacting their ability to move forward. To see someone and understand their reality in order to coach them, we must be present and observant. Who are we coaching? What are they trying to achieve? What's their situation? Our listening and inquiry at this first step are all about learning.

The second step is to "Align." Through coaching, we help someone imagine a different future just beyond the threshold. We engage our imaginations and consider all options, using careful thinking to assess the advantages and disadvantages of each course of action. As coaching sparks their curiosity, the possibilities will multiply. The important questions we ask at this step include, "Given where you think you want to go, what options do you have?" and "What route might be the best way forward?" Exploring these questions allows the future to factor into their decision-making.

We are always moving. Taking time with the first two steps of A^3 greatly increases the likelihood that the person's actions are moving them in the right direction. The third step of the A^3 Coaching Model—"Act"—involves laying out a strategy and making plans to move quickly, strategically, and with alignment. The questions we ask as we "act" are: What will you do? When will you do it by? Who will help? This step ensures shared clarity about success measures, as well as roles, responsibilities, and accountabilities.

The A^3 Coaching Model supports us in helping people own their experience, explore their challenge, solve their own problem, and move to purposeful action. Using the A^3 Coaching Model also helps us achieve the proof points we seek as leaders. We are creating alignment. We are building bench strength. We are coordinating action.

Aim:

- What is your situation?
- What is the best possible outcome?
- What's in your way?
- How may you be contributing to the status quo?
- What absolutely MUST happen?
- Can I give you some feedback?
    - Here's a strength I see that supports your success (do more of this).
    - Here's a behavior that may be holding you back (do less of this).

Align:

- What are your options?

- How does each option get you closer to your best possible outcome?

- What might you have to let go of or learn in order to achieve your best possible outcome?

Act:

- What will you do?

- What's the simplest, best next step?

- Whom do you need to engage for support?

- How can I support you?

Using the A³ Coaching Model, we remind ourselves and encourage the person we are coaching to think more carefully, to feel more fully, and to communicate more effectively. When we look to coach, we help the other person own their reality and accelerate their development in accordance with the five coaching tenets.

COACHING WITH TAPS

Using TAPs as a focal point for 1:1 meetings is a smart way to drive progress and reinforce individual accountability. This conversation design reframes your regular 1:1 into a coaching conversation. Remember, the 1:1 is not for you as the team leader; it's for your team member. Your team members don't need to be told what to do or how to do it. Team members do want and need to understand the larger context in which they are working, to see how their contribution is making an impact, and to get coaching and guidance on how they can improve.

Using the TAP as focal point for the 1:1 ensures you're talking about the right topics, making your 1:1 a more productive use of time. You're able to check on progress, celebrate successes, identify barriers, explore options to overcome barriers, and agree on next steps. That sure sounds like coaching to me.

Here's how the leaders and teams I work with structure 1:1s to be coaching sessions rather than report-outs on task lists:

- Before the 1:1, have your team member review their TAP and assess the current status of each action and outcome. They could use the same RAG color code we use for the Team Roadmap.

  - Green = On Track

  - Amber = Stuck/Options Exist/Need to Act

  - Red = Stuck/No Solution

- During the 1:1, there are six questions to ask.

  - **Looking at your current TAP, what's on track (green)?** By asking about recent "wins," we recognize both effort and achievement. We also grow our understanding of some positive aspects of individual and team performance.

  - **Where are you stuck (amber or red)?** Coach to help with problem-solving. Think A^3: What's the objective? What have you tried? What are your options? What might you do? What's your next best step?

  - **How are you progressing toward your development goals?** How is your progress or lack of progress impacting your ability to achieve your TAP actions and outcomes? What change to your development plan would keep you on track?

- **How can I help?** This is one of the most powerful coaching questions we can ask. Invite your direct report to let you know what they need more of or less of from you to help them achieve their objectives.

- **What suggestions or feedback do you have for me?** The evidence is clear. Leaders who seek feedback from their direct reports dramatically and more quickly increase in leadership effectiveness. It reinforces that the 1:1 is a dialogue and not an instruction session or status update. We help one another get better at our respective roles.

- **What are you going to do and when are you going to do it by?** Contracting for completion is a vital component of any coaching process. This two-part question establishes a promise of accountability.

These six questions align with the A^3 coaching model. Following this framework, you are helping each team member shape their next normal. They own their situation. Coaching communicates your belief that they have the solution within them. Your inquiry helps draw it out.

A NOTE ABOUT FEEDBACK

There will be times when you will have to provide feedback on how the person you're coaching is engaging and performing. When we coach, we assume the person we are coaching has the ability to engage and perform. If they are underperforming in some way, the first assumption should be there is some barrier in their way. Most likely, it is an external barrier that coaching can help them identify and overcome. Maybe they can't see the guiding stars you've set, or maybe they lack the provisions they need. Sometimes, it's an internal barrier, like a lack of skill or will.

The decision to share feedback with another person grows out of an intention to help them grow. Providing feedback is a crucial part of the coaching process because there is always a gap between what a team member intends and how they are perceived. We all have blind spots. In business and in life, these spots usually go unnoticed until someone who cares about us points them out to us. Who cares enough about us to tell us we have lettuce stuck in our teeth? Feedback is a vital tool in helping someone to mind the gap and shift their behavior.

Sometimes the feedback we share may be labeled and received as negative, but in actuality, all feedback is constructive. It's just that some feedback (feedback about a positive behavior) is easier to share, and some feedback (feedback about a limiting or counterproductive behavior) is more difficult to deliver. When we look to coach, we need the emotional intelligence to recognize any anxiety that delivering difficult feedback may produce for us and how receiving difficult feedback may be difficult for the person we are coaching.

COACHING: RETHINK, RESET, RENEW

Are you ready to be a good coach? Here's another spot where you can break out the journal and do some reflecting on your ability to engage your team to create the next normal and your readiness to shift to a coach approach. It's another chance to rethink in order to reset and create your next normal as a leader.

JOURNAL TIME

Think about each item on this list. Rate yourself on a scale of one to five, with one meaning this item is an aspiration for you and five meaning the item is true for you all the time.

Engaging Your Team

I provide a vision and clear strategy for my team.

1 2 3 4 5

I provide a clearly-defined work breakdown structure (RACI) for my team.

1 2 3 4 5

I model and expect personal accountability.

1 2 3 4 5

I do not micromanage my team members.

1 2 3 4 5

I value my team members intrinsically and not just for what they produce.

1 2 3 4 5

I focus on results and productivity.

1 2 3 4 5

I encourage and support the ongoing development of my team members.

1 2 3 4 5

I have the business acumen and technical skills to support my
team's efforts.

1   2   3   4   5

These items relate to Google's *Project Oxygen* list of behaviors
that encourage engagement. If your total score for these items is
thirty-three or above, you have a strong capacity for encouraging
your team's high engagement. You're creating alignment by communicating your vision and strategy. Your team understands their
roles and accountabilities. You are empowering others to own their
experience and results. Your people sense your concern for them,
as demonstrated through your balanced focus on the results they
deliver and on their ongoing personal, professional, and career
development.

If you scored between twenty-two and thirty-two, you are
inclined to encourage engagement; however, your focus on this
may be inconsistent. You may overly focus on tasks and transactions
versus balancing that with time spent on development and relationship management. If your scores are between eight and twenty-one, you and your team would benefit from you taking a more
balanced approach to leading them and focusing on helping them
come together and work together as a team—as much as on driving
toward results. It may be time to ask how this is working for you and
your team.

Coaching Your Team
I hold regular and frequent coaching conversations with my team
members.

1   2   3   4   5

I give timely and direct feedback to help others grow and perform better.

1   2   3   4   5

More often than not, when people bring me their problem, I coach them to find their own solution.

1   2   3   4   5

When coaching, I confirm the "what, when, and why" of the person's goals.

1   2   3   4   5

I publicly endorse the positive contributions of others.

1   2   3   4   5

When I give feedback, it is based on concrete examples of behavior.

1   2   3   4   5

I follow up with the people I coach to see how they are progressing toward their goals.

1   2   3   4   5

I seek coaching myself on a regular basis.

1   2   3   4   5

These items have to do with having a coaching mindset and using a coach approach to team leadership. If your scores add up to thirty-three or higher, you have a positive attitude toward coaching and employ a coach approach consistently. You have a strong understanding of the value of coaching and are working to put it to practice. You use inquiry to encourage others to own their reality and find their own solutions. You demonstrate concern for the development of others by providing feedback on a regular basis. Good for you.

If your scores are between twenty-two and thirty-two, you have room to shift your perspective on coaching and an opportunity to work on your coaching skillset. You may use a coach approach sporadically, seeing coaching as not the most convenient or expedient method for directing the activities of others. If your scores are between eight and twenty-one, a coach approach mindset may not be your default setting. Challenge yourself to explore this with a trusted advisor or your own coach.

As you create your next normal and the next normal for your team, is there more work for you to do to hone your coaching skills?

The answer for all of us is, "yes." The work of change on a macro, organizational level begins with and relies on change at a micro, individual level. Your people need to see a change in you in order to believe in your veracity and trust your determination when it comes to the organizational change you may be calling for. So, call for change. Create a team around you that is empowered to collaboratively model and lead that change. Bring them together and coach them to achieve their mission. By stepping into your own next normal, you enable your team to create their next normal.

How do we replicate and scale the mindset, skills, behaviors, and practices that enable organizational change? Turn the page.

THIS IS THE WAY

IN THE TV SERIES, *The Mandalorian*, Mando and the other Mandalorians follow a code that informs their decisions about how to be in the world. When they act according to their code, they say, "This is the way."

The leadership and team management system you're using communicates what you value and reinforces the behaviors you want to scale. By default or by design, you are always shaping the next normal, the new "way" for your team.

The principles, practices, and processes we've covered in these pages are a way to rethink, reset, and renew your leadership and shape the next normal for you, your team, and your organization. They represent a "way" of transformative leadership. Leading this way can ensure your next normal will be one where people and teams are aligned on what's most important, can shape their work and achieve their best, and do so in an environment of empowerment and accountability.

How do we create value? How do we organize and operate (to create value)?

Next Normal Leadership & Team Management System

Rethink, Reset, and Renew Your Impact.

Principles (Your Foundation and POV)

- The Organization Is a Living System
- Change Is Normative
- Leadership Is a Balancing Act
- Build Bridges, Not Walls
- You're a Coach, Not a Machine Operator
- To Win Is to Learn and to Serve

Practices (The Work of Transformative Leadership)

Align People

Build Bench Strength

Coordinate Action

Process (The Way to the Next Normal)

- Establish/Practice Team Commitments – Set, Measure, Review at Least Quarterly
- Build/Follow Team Roadmaps – Create Shared Clarity of Mission, Success Measures, Execution Plan, RACI – Conduct Regular RAG Review
- Activate with 90-Day Individual Tactical Action Plans (TAPs)
- Empower with 1:1 Coaching Framework using TAPs

Be a Good Coach (Engage. Empower. Activate.)

Coaching Mindset:

- Be Conscious
- Be Connected
- Be Concerned

Look to:

- Learn
- Make Positive Assumptions
- Use Inquiry Before Advocacy
- Enable Transformation: Don't Seek Information (Problem-Solve)
- Coach the Person, Not the Problem

SHAPING YOUR NEXT NORMAL

When I was an undergrad, one of my professors began every class by saying, "*Repetitio est mater studiorum*," which means, "Repetition is the mother of learning." He would then repeat the key ideas from the previous class he wanted us to remember; that was how we knew it was going to be on the test.

Let's recap the principles, practices, and processes that, when applied, enable you to shape a positive next normal for yourself, your team, and your organization.

Creating the next normal always entails solving two perennial questions: How are we driving value? and How are we running our business? How we answer these questions, especially the second one, depends on the principles informing how we see the organization, understand change, and approach leadership. My six key principles are:

1. The organization is not a machine; it's a living system full of human beings.

2. Change is normative.

3. Leading organizations filled with people takes a balanced approach.

4. You're a bridge-builder, not a wall-protector.

5. If you're a leader, you're a coach.

6. Winning means learning faster and sharing that knowledge in service of others.

With your principles providing the foundation for your work, what *is* your work? Your work is to align people, build bench strength, and coordinate action. When you do this, you create the conditions for the humans around you to engage, shape their work, and achieve their best. The practices and processes outlined in this book give you the tools you need in order to shape the next normal for you, your team, and your organization.

These principles, practices, and processes combine to form a team management system that helps your team come together and commit to working together in a productive way that generates trust, empowerment, and mutual accountability. Your team will align around its unique mission, shared goals, a plan for achieving those goals, and clarity of each person's role and responsibility to the team. You'll help each person shape their work by focusing their attention and time on the most important outcomes they can produce, and you'll help each person achieve their best by coaching them to own their contribution and development. This is the way to your team's next normal.

NINETY DAYS TO YOUR NEXT NORMAL

If you're serious about shaping and sustaining a next normal with your team, start by following the Ninety Days to Your Next Normal framework. This is the sequence and timeline the leaders I coach follow.

Month One:

- Get clear on the impact you want to have and write your Impact Statement. Decide what noticeable change you'll make, so your team knows you're serious when you talk about what's changing.

- Get clear on your messaging. What's the mission you want the team to align around? Get used to repeating this message over and over again.

- Consider the stakeholders and constituencies with whom you and your team need to engage in order to accomplish your mission. Set a plan to enroll them and secure their support.

- Evaluate the current state of the team using the Teamwork GPS framework (Guiding Stars, Provisions, and Skill and Will).

- Have a 1:1 with each team member to get to know them better. Have the team member do some version of the Impact Statement exercise. This helps you learn how you can help each team member with their development.

Month Two:

- Engage your team in conversations to reset and shape the next normal. These conversations could take place over three days in-person or over two to three weeks if conducted virtually.

- Conversation 1: facilitate connection. Convene a meeting with the team to facilitate connecting. There's no other agenda—the purpose is for the team to connect. Even if everyone knows one another, this is time well spent. I like a simple exercise where each person shares ten things about themselves that others may not know. Another option is for the team to share their Impact Statements with one another.

- Conversation 2: define high team performance. Convene a meeting to define high team performance and make commitments to meet your definition.

- Ask each team member to identify a development goal related to your new team commitments. Ask team members to engage in some 1:1s with one another to gather suggestions and get coaching for how to work toward their development goal.

- Conversation 3: convene a meeting to create alignment using the Team Roadmap tool. If you're meeting in person, allow up to two days to create your first Roadmap. If meeting virtually, here's how most teams convene these conversations.

  □ Step 1. State the team's mission. Invite the team to share their ideas and determine the success measures (outcomes and metrics) for your specified timeframe. Allow ninety minutes to two hours for this conversation.

  □ Step 2. Select stewards. Identify which team member will serve as steward for each outcome. Request each steward convene a meeting with a subset of the team to look more closely at the draft workstream. Allow sixty minutes for this conversation.

  □ Step 3. Allow the steward time to convene their group to generate a first cut of the big rocks. Identifying the big rocks may take three hours if you're meeting in person or require one to three meetings if the group is working virtually. If each steward's group is working virtually, allow one to two weeks for this work to occur.

  □ Step 4. Review the work of each steward's small group and create alignment on the completed Team Roadmap. Allow ninety minutes to two hours for this conversation.

Conversation 4: convene a meeting with the team to discuss the governance cadence and process for staying aligned, keeping commitments, and coordinating all work. This is where you lay out how you'll review your Team Roadmap regularly, revisit your team commitments to maintain bench strength, and request each team member generate their individual TAP to focus work and drive progress.

Month Three:

- Set 1:1s with each team member to review their TAPs, confirm alignment on their outcomes, and commit to mutual accountability.

- Convene your first monthly Roadmap review meeting using the RAG process.

What should you expect by implementing this system with your leadership team? You should expect a more connected, more aligned, more empowered team acting with greater intentionality when navigating through constant change. These ninety days are only the beginning of shaping your next normal, but you can use the processes in this book as you sustain and scale what you've begun.

90 Days to Your Team's Next Normal

1. Generate Your Impact Statement (Change begins with you.)

2. Determine Team Starting Point (Use Teamwork GPS to assess current state.)

3. Remember Stages of Team Development (Forming, Storming, Norming, Performing)

4. Bring Team Together to Connect (Forming)

5. Establish Team Commitments (Storming to Decide Team Norms)

6. Align People around Team Roadmap (Create Shared Clarity of Mission, Success Measures, Execution Plan, RACI.)

7. Activate team members with 90-Day Individual Tactical Action Plans (TAPs)

8. Set Cadence for Team Roadmap & Commitments Reviews and Coaching 1:1s using TAPs

SUSTAINING MOMENTUM

Adopting and applying this team management system strengthens alignment and empowers people and teams. Aligned and empowered teams are resilient teams. Earlier, we talked about becoming unsinkable, being able to learn, adapt, and act quickly in an always-changing environment. That's what resilience is all about: being able to bounce back from challenges more capable and confident than before. The more resilient we are, the more focused, creative, and effective we are at approaching and succeeding in our work.

We don't become more resilient through willpower. We become and stay resilient by building routines and rituals into our regular experience. Sustaining what you've begun with your team will require routines and rituals that keep you aligned, focused on the right work, and committed to engaging one another in productive ways.

This way of transformative leadership will require an intentional investment of your time, energy, and resources. What will you get in return? That depends on what you're after. Your next normal is for you to shape. What we do know is that when leaders adhere to these principles and work to align people, build bench strength, and coordinate action, their teams become more engaged and better able to navigate and lead organizational transformation. Stronger alignment and more coordinated action reduce cycle time to make decisions, deliver solutions, and create value. Continuous focus on building bench strength reinforces the importance of intentional individual and collective development.

To sustain what you begin, set a cadence of regular team conversations and coach each team member to engage in conversations on the right topics in the right way. Review your Team Roadmap and your team commitments at least quarterly, if not monthly. Set a regular cadence of 1:1s with each team member to review their TAPs.

DRIVING STRATEGIC CULTURE CHANGE

You are instigating a shift from prior operating principles, practices, and processes to a new way of leading and guiding teams in order to create value and achieve a sustained competitive advantage. The decision to shape the next normal begins a journey to produce strategic culture change. The question becomes, "Do you want to put some intention behind that decision or just hope for the best?"

Larry Senn, founder of Senn-Delany and "the Father of Corporate Culture," sees four pieces critical to successful culture shaping. First, the leadership team owns and drives the process. "Do as I say, not as I do" is a terrible parenting strategy; it also dooms change efforts to failure when it is the posture of the leadership team. Second, each leader models and calls for personal change. If you're calling for change, your people need to see how *you're changing*. If they don't see a change in how you show up and lead, they won't believe you're serious about them having to change. Third, broad engagement encourages acceptance, adoption, and application of the new paradigm. Engage enthusiasts and influencers from across the organization as ambassadors for change in order to achieve critical mass. To scale any change, use the change checklist to generate your strategy and plan to engage your organization. Fourth, leaders create a platform for systematic reinforcement over time to embed the ways of the new culture. How you communicate about change and for how long will be a significant determinant of success. And, actions speak louder than words.

Perhaps your organization conducts quarterly business reviews (QBRs). Those meetings, on a regular cadence, keep people informed on the status and progress of your organization's important work. Driving strategic culture shift as part of your organizational transformation requires similar communication events. A number of our clients establish a communications platform with large-group forums and small-group connect sessions. These events serve to sustain alignment, encourage individual and collective development of the skills and behaviors critical to success moving forward, and maintain a high level of coordination as the organization makes its way forward. These events become important touch points for sharing information, securing feedback on the current state and progress, and generating ideas from leaders critical to ensuring your change efforts succeed.

The leader and leadership team are seen driving these events as part of the organizational change effort. They share stories of their personal journeys navigating change and managing transition. They are open about how they're learning along with everyone else. They're modeling the behaviors they want to scale as part of the strategic culture shift that eventually changes how they run their business and create value. They're creating an organization that excels at the work of transformation.

When scaled to multiple teams across an organization, this team management system facilitates cross-functional, multilevel communication and feedback, making the organization more adaptable, quicker to learn, and better able to maintain pace and progress. You are leading a strategic culture shift, transforming yourself, your team, and your organization in the process. I think you've made it this far because you want to be intentional about how you lead. You don't want to just find yourself in a new normal; you want to create your next normal. The approach outlined in these pages provides a means to turn your intention into action.

ONE MORE THING...

Have you ever heard the story of the old carpenter? When he told his employer of his plans to retire and live a more leisurely life with his wife and family, his employer asked if he could build just one more house as a personal favor. The carpenter said, "Yes," but in time, it was easy to see that his heart was not in his work. He cut corners and used inferior materials. He was not building something he would be proud of; he was "ticking a box."

When the carpenter finished his work, and his employer came to inspect the house, the employer handed the front-door key to the carpenter. "This is your house," he said. "It's my gift to you." What a shock! What a shame! If the carpenter had only known he was building his own house, he would have done it all so differently. Now, he had to live in the home he had built none too well.

So it is with us. We can build our lives in a distracted way, reacting rather than acting, willing to put up less than the best. Then, with a shock, we look at the situation we have created and find we are now living in the house we have built. If we had realized that, we would have done it differently.

Think of yourself as the carpenter. Each day, you hammer a nail, place a board, or erect a wall. Build wisely. It is the only life you will ever build. Even if you live it for only one day more, that day deserves to be lived graciously and with dignity. After all, life is a do-it-yourself project.

The choices you make shape your next normal and the next normal for your team and your organization. Choose wisely, for you own the experience you create and the results you produce. Indeed, the choices we make each day about how to show up and lead determine our impact and our legacy.

We'll end where we began, with the words of poet and activist Amanda Gorman, who writes, "Let us not return to what was normal, but reach toward what is next." Leaders enable positive transformation. That's what you signed up for. You're at the point of no return. There's no turning back. The shape of your next normal is up to you. Keep going. Keep reaching. You've got this.

ACKNOWLEDGMENTS

I'VE BEEN THE BENEFICIARY of the wisdom and generosity of innumerous teachers, colleagues, and leaders who have been part of my journey. The lessons I've learned by paying careful attention and endeavoring to emulate and amplify the wisdom these people impart through their words and deeds have made me a better person, a better coach, and have hopefully found their way into these pages. I am a conduit, a curator, a connector of dots, doing my best to synthesize and articulate what my insatiable appetite for learning and growth has amassed so far. I am indebted to them all.

Marshall Goldsmith and I have never met in person (yet). And, through his writing and work, I consider him a mentor and *bodhisattva*. He is a true teacher who inspires me to be authentic, light, unattached, and generous.

Over a decade ago, it was my good fortune to meet an amazing woman, coach, and consultant, Pat Newmann, *"your partner in change."* The chance to work with Pat, laugh with Pat, and learn from Pat was incredibly impactful. Pat engages with everyone with a fierce authenticity and gentle elegance. She has forgotten more about coaching, leadership, and change than the rest of us will ever know. Every moment with Pat is a masterclass.

I would be absolutely lost without Sina Johnson. They say it takes a village; Sina is an entire village. She runs operations at Giuliano Associates. And she does so much more than that. She is a thinking partner, motivator, teacher who is always ready, willing, and able to make my next crazy idea a reality. Most importantly, with Sina, everything is easy, uncomplicated, and fun.

The team that has helped bring this book to life has been incredible. Emily Gindlesparger, Chas Hoppe, Hussein Albaiaty, Bianca Pahl, and the rest of the team at Scribe Media are stars.

Finally, I want to express my eternal gratitude to the many leaders and teams who have allowed me the privilege to walk with them for a time, support their aspirations, and contribute what I could to their important work. Your willingness to go to the edge and push farther challenges and inspires me to do the same. Here's to what's next!

Made in the USA
Middletown, DE
08 June 2022

66871564R00076